Teresa —
Never (
your ...

UNLEASH
your
BRAVERY

Saying YES to Jesus, Even When You Are Afraid

Unleash Your Bravery
Saying Yes to Jesus, Even When You Are Afraid
Copyright © 2024 by Heidi Nicole Elizarraraz

Scripture quotations marked NIV are taken from the Holy Bible, New International Version NIV. Copyright 1973, 1978, 1984, 2011 by Biblica, Inc. Used by permission of Zondervan. All rights reserved worldwide. Scripture quotations marked NLT are taken from the Holy Bible, New Living Translation, copyright 1996, 2004, 2007, 2013 by Tyndale House Foundation. Used by permission of Tyndale House Publishers, Inc., Carol Stream, Illinois 60188. All rights reserved.Scripture quotations marked ESV are taken from The Holy Bible, English Standard Version. ESV Text Edition: 2016. Copyright 2001 by Crossway Bibles, a publishing ministry of Good News Publishers.
Scripture quotations marked (NASB) are taken from the New American Standard Bible Copyright 1960, 1971, 1977, 1995 by The Lockman Foundation. All rights reserved.

Front & Back Cover Design by Sergio Gomez
Interior Book Design by Alex P. Johnson

ISBN 13
978-1-63132-234-1
Library of Congress Control Number: 2024911029
Library of Congress Cataloging-in-Publication Data
is available upon request.

First Edition

Published in the United States of America by ALIVE Book Publishing
an imprint of Advanced Publishing LLC
3200 A Danville Blvd., Suite 204, Alamo, California 94507
alivebookpublishing.com

PRINTED IN THE UNITED STATES OF AMERICA

10 9 8 7 6 5 4 3 2 1

UNLEASH
your
BRAVERY

SAYING YES TO JESUS,
EVEN WHEN YOU ARE AFRAID

Heidi Nicole Elizarraraz

ABOOKS
Alive Book Publishing

Watch, stand fast in the faith, be brave, be strong.
~ 1 Corinthians 16:13 NTV

ACKNOWLEDGEMENTS

I want to acknowledge my husband, Daniel Elizarraraz, who has always encouraged me to dream big and to unleash my bravery as God calls me deeper with Him. He has believed in me and empowered me to say Yes to Jesus, even when I am afraid.

To my mom, DeAnn Eastman, who has always been my biggest cheerleader, prayer warrior, and friend. She was the first person to read these words and to courageously believe God for the calling on my life, even if it meant losing me to another country.

Pastors Doug and Crystal Heisel, thank you for believing in us, championing us, and supporting us since day one. You saw something in us that we didn't even see in ourselves, and you called us higher. Open Arms wouldn't be what it is today without your prayers and support. New Life Church has made an incredible impact on our ministry. We are forever grateful.

Thank you to my wonderful editor, Roz Goodall, who voluntarily stood in the gap for me and this work and encouraged me on every chapter. You have made my words come to life. Thank you for your generosity of time and expertise. You are truly an answered prayer from the Lord.

Special appreciation to Abril Fonseca, whose tireless dedication to translating this work into Spanish and whose unwavering support from our humble beginnings, when our pockets held only a dollar, has been invaluable. Your commitment to going above and beyond is deeply appreciated.

Heartfelt thanks to the dedicated team and families of Open Arms, whose love and support have provided a firm foundation from which to conquer fears and embrace bravery. Together, we have chosen the journey of saying yes to Jesus each day.

Gratitude to our sponsors and generous supporters whose belief in our vision of keeping families together has been instrumental in ensuring that no child faces the hardship of being home alone or left abandoned. Your generosity has made a profound difference in the lives of many.

To the members of our church community, especially the women of ELLA (SHE), who have welcomed and nurtured me, guiding me from insecurity to boldness and bravery. Together, we have faced our fears and emerged stronger.

Lastly, to my Lord Jesus, the true hero of this story. Without You, I am nothing. All glory and honor belong to You. Thank You for choosing me and instilling in me the courage to walk boldly in Your path. You are my everything.

My heartfelt gratitude,
Heidi Elizarraraz

To learn more or to support our mission, please visit:
OpenArmsMexico.org

You can also connect with the author at:
UnleashYourBravery.com

CONTENTS

FOREWORD

It happens to all of us. Our hearts beat faster, our palms get sweaty, and our knees go weak. From the most seasoned saint to the newest believer, there are times when fear seems like the most tangible presence in the room, even for those of us who love Jesus with all our hearts. Fear bullies us and calls us cowards. It tells us that shrinking back and playing it safe are surely the most prudent things to do.

Fear and I have had our own stare-downs through the years. How I wish I'd had Heidi Elizarraraz's book, *Unleash Your Bravery: Saying Yes to Jesus, Even When You are Afraid*, in my arsenal back then. I'm glad I have it now. With beautifully written anecdotes and powerful stories from her own remarkable faith journey, Heidi reminds us that being brave doesn't require the absence of fear, or that we feel strong and in control. Bravery happens when our love for Jesus and others unleashes the courage to say that next, hard "yes" to Jesus, even when we don't know where it will take us.

With honest vulnerability, mingled with a relentless trust in her faithful God, Heidi pulls back the curtain and shows us what it's been like to pioneer and sustain a thriving ministry in Mexico that gives hope to poverty orphans and keeps families together, despite unfathomable obstacles and hardships. Like me, you'll probably shed a tear or two as you read *Unleash Your Bravery*. But even more importantly, you will discover fresh ways to face down fear, release your courage, and say that next, all-in "yes" to Jesus. Read on and let your own new season of bravery begin!

— Dr. Jodi Detrick, Coach, mentor, speaker, and author of *The Settled Soul* and *The Jesus-Hearted Woman*, former columnist for *The Seattle Times*

.

DEDICATION

This book is dedicated to my two world-changing daughters, Samaria and Selah. Your unwavering inspiration has propelled me to pen these pages, crafting a legacy not just for you but for the generations you will bring forth.

In the tapestry of our family history, the narrative is woven with threads of profound faith. It commenced with my great uncle Everett West, accepting Jesus, and encountering the Holy Spirit at the Azusa Street Revival that transformed the trajectory of our lineage. Through him, my great grandfather, William B. West, had an encounter with Jesus. My family's resounding yes to Jesus set into motion a legacy of pastors, missionaries, worship leaders, educators, and devoted followers of Christ. Samaria and Selah, that same legacy courses through your veins.

It's a legacy of wholehearted love for Jesus, prompting a fervent desire to proclaim His name far and wide until every soul encounters Him. For generations, our family has embraced the ethos of making Jesus' last command our first priority (Mark 16:15). My precious daughters, it is my fervent prayer that you and your children will uphold and further this legacy that honors God.

You are also personally blessed to have a God-fearing earthly father, who has said yes to Jesus over and over. Although his story is one of growing up in an orphanage in Mexico where he suffered much and missed his parents. Someone stood up to fight for his well-being. And now, he fights so others do not have the same life he once endured. He is a valiant warrior, like Gideon in the book of Judges, who's brave pioneering steps have broken generational curses and paved a way for your future.

I want to encourage you both, that in moments when fear, worry, or anxiety threaten to obscure your path and hinder God's unfolding plan, remember this: you both possess profound bravery. You have the power to echo a resounding YES to Jesus, even in the face of fear. May this book serve as your compass, a constant reminder that diving wholeheartedly into God's plans is an endeavor eternally worthwhile. Holy Spirit, world-changing blood runs through your veins. Never let fear paralyze God's plans for your life.

To my incredibly brave daughters, you are the epitome of courage. I love you dearly and eagerly anticipate witnessing the incredible journey God has charted for you. Unleash your bravery, my courageous daughters. Be strong and courageous, for the Lord is with you.

With all my love,
Mom

Watch, stand fast in the faith, be brave, be strong.
~ 1 Corinthians 16:13 NTV

INTRODUCTION

FOR THE LAST TWENTY YEARS, I have been a missionary to Mexico. It has been the joy of my life to walk the dirt roads and fight to keep families together. I may be American but my heart beats Mexican. God has given me a love for this land and its people.

It is within these pages that my story unfolds, a narrative etched with encounters that span deserts of doubt, mountains of triumph, and oceans of grace. Welcome to a journey that delves into overcoming fear, and embracing courage as I began to follow Jesus and go "all-in" with His plans and purposes for my life.

This book is a testament to the transformative power of saying yes to God's call, even when it echoes in the corridors of fear. From the windswept deserts where uncertainty reigns to the radiant peaks where faith stands unshakable, these pages encapsulate a voyage marked by leaps of faith, devastating tragedies, and unexpected turns.

Meet the characters—the border bullies, the fears, the inadequacies, and the refining fires—each playing a crucial role in the grand narrative of surrender. As we traverse through these chapters, anticipate moments of vulnerability, triumphs of faith, and the pulsating heartbeat of a soul relentlessly pursuing the call of God in my life.

This is more than a recounting of personal experiences. It's an invitation—an invitation to embrace a life fully surrendered to God's plan for your life, even if fear comes knocking. Through the highs and lows, the triumphs and tribulations, a call to bravery emerges—an assurance that, even in the face of fear, you can navigate the realms of uncertainty with a resounding yes to God.

As we journey through these pages together, may you find echoes of your own story, gather courage to face your fears, and discover that an all-in life is the grandest adventure of all. So, let us turn the page and step into the narrative of faith together, trusting that being brave isn't living without fear, it's saying yes to Jesus even when you are afraid.

Be strong and courageous. Do not fear or be in dread of them, for it is the Lord your God who goes with you. He will not leave you or forsake you. ~ Deuteronomy 31:6 (ESV)

Be strong, and let your heart take courage, all you who wait for the Lord! ~ Psalm 31:24 (ESV)

Chapter 1
Be Strong and Courageous:
Facing Your Fears

Have I not commanded you? Be strong and courageous. Do not be afraid; do not be discouraged, for the Lord your God will be with you wherever you go. ~ Joshua 1:9, NIV

"YES, I'LL GO TO MEXICO on a mission trip with you; I want to practice my Spanish." When I said this, little did I know how this one sentence would utterly change my life.

My existence revolved around the echo of "me, me, and me." I was immersed in self-improvement, aiming for a double major and a minor from college. My motivation? Success. Graduating with Spanish as a major, I envisioned myself as a prominent reporter or a bilingual motivational speaker. Mexico was merely a pitstop to polish my Spanish skills.

Little did I know, my life was about to take an unexpected turn.

In a small Mexican village, distributing church service flyers became my agenda. Roaming the dirt roads, my mission was singular—to practice my Spanish. It wasn't about ushering them to church or being a witness; my intentions were self-centered—until I encountered a girl who altered the course of my life. Candelaria, a seven-year-old with worn shoes and tattered clothes, looked at me with eyes that seemed to pierce my very soul.

Kneeling to her eye level, I felt her silent plea to be seen, loved, and freed from the shackles of fear and uncertainty. Ironically, I, a white, blonde, soon-to-be college graduate, saw myself mirrored in her circumstances.

Was it the desire to matter to someone; the pain concealed in

Uncomfortable and trying to enhance my Spanish, God spoke, redirecting me to my destiny and life's calling.

her eyes; the apprehension of an unknown future? Time seemed to freeze as I locked eyes with her, feeling seen for the first time. I didn't want to leave, but I also didn't want to intrude, so I continued distributing the flyers.

As I walked away from Candelaria, I heard God's voice for the first time—a Moses-and-the-burning-bush moment. It was a voice of love, breaking through the noise when I stepped out of my comfort zone. Uncomfortable and trying to enhance my Spanish, God spoke, redirecting me to my destiny and life's calling.

At that crossroads, God's voice, full of love, presented me with two paths. I could pursue worldly success, fulfilling my dreams, or embrace a different plan. God's plan. He reminded me of Jeremiah 29:11 NIV; *"For I know the plans I have for you, declares the Lord. Plans to prosper you and not to harm you, plans to give you a hope and a future."* He declared, "Heidi, this is the plan I have for you. This is why you studied Spanish. THIS [Mexico] is your destiny. *Come, follow me"* (Matthew 4:19 NIV). As

I had to say yes, to go all-in with His plans and purposes for my life, even in the face of fear.

God continued to speak to me, he emphasized, "You can't have one foot in the world and one foot in with me. You need to go all-in."

All-in—those words echoed through my ears like a cymbal.

For too long, I confused religion with a relationship with God. Claiming to be a Christian, I wasn't living like one. This encounter forced a revelation: I lacked a personal relationship with Jesus Christ. I was following selfish desires instead of following God.

Since that moment with Jesus, I've never been the same.

Uncontrollable tears flowed during the trip as I could no longer run or hide. I couldn't say *no* to His voice, to His calling on my life, even though the ramifications of saying *yes* terrified me. His voice was loving, tender, and full of wonder. I had to say *yes*, to go all-in with His plans and purposes for my life, even in the face of fear.

God's Plan Is Better Than Our Own Plan

The next day marked the end of the mission trip. The journey back from Tecate, in Baja California, to Visalia, California, felt like a pivotal stretch. My college roommate, Rachel, eager for our grand move to Los Angeles, called me with news of an apartment. "Heidi, I found an apartment. When you get home, I just need you to come and co-sign for it," she excitedly declared. The weight of my decision loomed large at that moment. Would I dismiss the clear message God had given me because I was afraid to relinquish it all, hesitant to truly follow God's will? Or would I cast fear aside and say *yes* to God? The decision crystallized within me. Taking a deep breath, I replied, "Rachel, I am so sorry. You are going to have to look for another roommate. I am moving to Mexico." The car's occupants turned to me, eyebrows raised, mouth agape, seeking confirmation. It was true. I had heard God's voice, and I had decided to follow Him.

> ...your life can transform significantly if you summon the courage to say yes to God, even in the face of fear.

To be utterly transparent, the weight of my *yes* was daunting. Have you ever felt the grip of fear—that paralyzing sensation escalating your heartbeat, making your palms sweat, and sending your thoughts into a tailspin? Fear is a natural emotion, yet it can also be incapacitating. It has the potential to hinder you from embracing the life God has beckoned you to, from taking risks, and from stepping out in faith. But fear cannot dictate the course of your life.

Consider this: your life can transform significantly if you summon the courage to say yes to God, even in the face of fear. At twenty two, fresh out of college, if someone had asked me what my life would look like in twenty years, I wouldn't have envisioned living on the dusty roads of Mexico surrounded by children while fighting daily to keep them off the streets and out of orphanages.

This wasn't part of my plan. It wasn't my dream. It wasn't the life I had imagined. Yet, I am profoundly thankful that God's plans and dreams for my life exceeded my own. It still boggles my mind that God would choose me to be His hands and feet in Mexico—me, with my ample flaws and seemingly insurmountable fear. Surely, God could have chosen someone more qualified, more experienced, less sinful, and far less terrified. But for reasons beyond my understanding, He chose me, embracing my past, forgiving my sins, and calming my fears.

Fear That Masquerades

Fear, that dirty four-letter word. That emotion we deal with often, especially when God asks us to say yes to following Him. Fear is that unpleasant emotion caused by the belief that someone or something is dangerous, likely to be a threat or cause pain.[1]

Yes, fear is undeniably unpleasant, capable of holding you back from uttering that resounding yes to Jesus. It has shadowed me throughout my life, seeping into my childhood, adolescence, and adulthood, even onto the mission field where I serve God in full-time ministry. Every time God nudges me toward a new endeavor, fear attempts to creep in, an eerie dark shadow hanging over me. It has tried to keep me from saying yes to Jesus and fulfilling my God-designed destiny. Has fear ever tried to stifle your yes too?

Trying to pinpoint the genesis of fear in my life proved elusive. Did it embed itself when my parents fought during the silent hours of the night, or was it during that fateful family trip to the lake when I was molested? Perhaps it was the seismic shift when my parents divorced as I entered high school, turning my life upside down. Or was it when financial struggles cast their long shadows, and we could barely make ends meet?

The exact moment when fear became my companion remains unclear. As a child, I grew up in a Christian home, attending church every Sunday with my mom and siblings. I participated in church, and was baptized, ready to follow Jesus for a lifetime—until my parents divorced when I turned thirteen. That's when anxiety, like a sudden gust, began to churn in my stomach, stealing my breath away. Fear of the unknown loomed large, and worry became my unwelcome companion.

Worry, the mind dwelling on difficulties and troubles, shifted my focus from Jesus to my circumstances. Petrified of this new chapter in my life, I even worried myself into an ulcer. I was the Christian friend, the one whose parents were still together, but now *my* family was being torn apart. Fear, masquerading as worry and doubt, rushed in. I feared my mom wouldn't have enough finances to care for us without my dad's help. I even curled up on my bed to do my homework with a flashlight to save on the electric bill, oblivious to the fact that batteries probably cost more.

I feared the unknown. I feared not having enough.

Instead of turning to God amid the trauma, I sought solace in friends and worldly pursuits, drifting away from God. I got entangled in the world's expectations, succumbing to its whispers—college choices, earning potential, car models, and brand name clothing. I wanted it all, believing it would alleviate the pain and quell the anxiety.

My life became self-centered, focused on self-sufficiency.

I mastered self-reliance to avoid depending on anyone else. Yet, deep down, it was just a façade camouflaging the underlying unease. I feared not being successful, not measuring up to the world's standards. I was confident but insecure, and being insecure is a lack of faith. Sin turned my focus inward, away from God, but even then, I couldn't ignore God's call. I applied to work at the orphanage I had visited on a mission trip, finished summer school, and graduated from college, and three months later took the leap of faith to move to Mexico. I told God, "I will give you one year of my life." That was over twenty years ago.

Before leaving to follow Jesus with everything I had, I faced significant backlash. God had spoken to me, but not everyone in my life had heard His voice. As I shared my encounter with Jesus and my decision to move to Mexico to work at an orphanage, the struggle intensified. It felt like everyone was against me—friends, my boyfriend, some of my family. They questioned, "How can you give up your hard-fought college career to make a dollar an hour in Mexico? How can you move to a third-world country? Do you even know what you'll be doing? Will you have a washer or a dryer?"

> I was confident but insecure, and being insecure is a lack of faith.

I lacked answers to their questions. All I knew was that I stood on the threshold of my Promised Land, prepared to follow God's plans and not my own. As Bruce Wilkinson calls them in his book *The Dream Giver*, I encountered "border bullies"—those who threaten to quash your dreams and push you back into your comfort zone.[2]

Surprisingly hurtful as it was, the experience echoed the challenges faced by the

> I told God, "I will give you one year of my life." That was over twenty years ago.

Israelites fleeing Egypt toward their Promised Land. In Numbers 13, we see Moses send the twelve spies into the land of Canaan. The land that God had promised that they would conquer. The land that flowed with milk and honey. The Lord had told Moses to send some men to explore the land that the Lord was going to give to the Israelites. Moses had to send a leader from each tribe as a representative. These twelve leaders, or spies, went to the land of Canaan, also called the Promised Land, that God was going to give to the Israelites. They went to spy before they could go and conquer it. The men were going to return with some fruits of the land because the land that flows with milk and honey is not called that for nothing, right? When they got back from spying, they gave Moses their report.

The twelve spies admitted that the land flowed with milk and honey, and they recognized that the fruit of Canaan was great and beautiful (Numbers 13:27), but ten out of twelve commented that the land was full of giants that would be impossible to defeat (Numbers 13:28, 31). They allowed the presence of the giants to diminish the value of God's promises because they were scared. Fear, that dirty four-letter word, came crashing in on them. They dreaded the giants. Maybe they feared that God would not hold true to His promise to give this land to their descendants (Exodus 33:1).

How many times have I been afraid that what God promised me wouldn't come to pass? Aren't we like the Israelites all too often? I know I am.

Defeating Your Border Bullies

Thankfully, in this Promised Land story, there were two men, Joshua and Caleb, who brought good reports full of faith and trust in God. Caleb spoke with confidence, saying, *"Let's go at once to take the land . . . We can certainly conquer it!"* (Numbers 13:30 NLT).

The ten spies thought the giants in Canaan were too large to conquer, but Joshua and Caleb knew that their God was too big to fail. Joshua and Caleb were the only two men who were positive in the face of the giants' opposition. They didn't ignore the challenges, but they didn't overemphasize them either . . . and they were the only ones out of all the spies who entered the Promised Land.

The spies who perished in the desert only saw what was and failed to envision what could be. Their fears eclipsed their faith, transforming them into border bullies hindering Moses and the Israelites from their Promised Land. Their negativity and complaints birthed defeatist attitudes, attempting to convince Moses that God's promises were untrue and that possessing the Promised Land was impossible.

> The spies who perished in the desert only saw what was and failed to envision what could be. Their fears eclipsed their faith,...

Your border bullies will exaggerate the dangers when you want to pursue God's plan for your life. Let's look at Scripture to see how the border bullies operate.

And they spread among the Israelites a bad report about the land they had explored, saying, "The land we explored devours those living in it. All the people we saw there are of great size." ~ Numbers 13:32 NIV

They exaggerated the dangers of the presence of the giants and gave a bad report to thousands of people, inciting fear in them.

Border bullies complain about the difficulties. They gave Moses this account:

We went into the land to which you sent us . . . But the people who live there are powerful, and the cities are fortified and very large. ~ Numbers 13:27-28 NIV

I know when I have complained about something God has called me to do, it has never convinced me to say yes to God. It has only discouraged me.

Pastor Bill Johnson from Bethel Church once said, "If God inhabits our praises, who inhabits our complaining? Complaining elevates the problem to where it has greater influence than faith." Complaining comes from the other camp, and it is what the devil uses to discourage you to lean into fear, and not to follow God's will for your life.

Border bullies also idealize the "good old days":

And again, the Israelites started wailing and said, "If only we had meat to eat! . . . But now we have lost our appetite; we never see anything but this manna." ~ Numbers 11:4 & 6 NIV

These antagonists remind you of your past and devalue what God has said about your present and your future. The people who discourage you want to keep you in your comfort zone because they are too fearful to leave their own.

It felt like the people closest to me were my biggest

> When God has called you to step out of your comfort zone and to say yes to Him, don't be surprised if border bullies come your way.

obstacles to overcome, and it may be similar for you. When God has called you to step out of your comfort zone and to say yes to Him, don't be surprised if border bullies come your way. Just remember what the Apostle Paul reminds us about in Ephesians 6:12 NIV; *"For our struggle is not against flesh and blood, but against the rulers, against the authorities, against the powers of this dark world and against the spiritual forces of evil in the heavenly realms."* Satan wants to use these coercers to discourage you in your calling and to doubt God's call on your life. Just remember that your fight is not against them but against Satan, who wants to *steal, kill, and destroy* God's plan for your life (John 10:10 NIV).

The people who discourage you the most deal with fear manifesting in themselves. In turn, their fearfulness gets placed on you. These are the people the enemy tries to use to prevent you from stepping foot into your Promised Land.

When the border bullies approached my camp, I internalized their fear, and other anxieties arose inside of me. I dreaded letting my friends and family down and wasting all the hard work I fought to accomplish in college. I also feared that my past of being a "party girl" would affect my future. How could I work at a Mexican orphanage and change a child's life with all the baggage and sin that consumed me?

I risked letting everyone down if I went, but I risked letting God down if I stayed. I was truly at a crossroads in my life. If I said yes to God's call on my life, I would have to sacrifice everything. I would have to break up with my boyfriend, who probably thought he was going to marry me. I would have to leave a well-paying job, and forgo my college degrees, which I had fought to earn while working full-time. I would have to give up my dream of becoming a news reporter. I would have to sell everything, even my brand-new Mustang, my dream car that I had just purchased.

> When did we start believing God wants to send us to safe places to do easy things, anyway?

The struggle was real.

Was God's plan for my life worth relinquishing all this? It was a daunting question, and fear loomed large.

Kick Fear in the Face

Trusting in God's call on my life has empowered me to confront fear head-on. I have learned that it *is* worth all the risk and all the sacrifice. When did we start believing God wants to send us to safe places to do easy things, anyway? When did we start believing that in order to proceed in God's calling, all fear must flee? Fear is there. It is real—very real. But I have learned that you can say yes to Jesus even if you are afraid.

Just when I think I've conquered my fear, God beckons me to go deeper, higher, farther. He calls me to step out of that warm and cozy comfort zone, and, unfortunately, terror sometimes creeps back in. Yet, on this journey of saying yes to God, I've discovered that sometimes I just have to do it scared. That's the essence of bravery. At times, I need to put one foot in front of the other until faith rises, and fear diminishes. I hold onto the truth that, *"God has not given me the spirit of fear, but of power, and of love, and of a sound mind"* (2 Timothy 1:7 KJV). Knowing it is one thing; living it out takes consistent, daily practice.

Sometimes I can kick fear in the face, and occasionally fear beats me up.

But here's the message: what you've done before doesn't have to dictate your future. I'm just an ordinary person like you, with many faults. We all desire to achieve something significant in this world, and when we allow the Holy Spirit to dwell in us, He accomplishes great things through us! He takes the ordinary and does something extraordinary. He even uses our past, turning it into His glory. His love helps us defeat the border bullies and overcome fears and anxiety; *"Such love has no fear, because perfect love expels all fear"* (1 John 4:18, NTV).

> Sometimes I can kick fear in the face, and occasionally fear beats me up.

Regardless of how far off the path you've gone, surrendering your life to Him and depending on Him carves a new path from where you were to where you should be. It's never too late. *"The gifts and calling of God are irrevocable"* (Romans 11:29 NET). God has used my past and mistakes to glorify Him, and if He's done it for me, He will do it for you. Unleash your bravery, dear reader, trust in the Lord, and take that step out of your comfort zone into your Promised Land. Remember the words the Lord spoke to Joshua as he was about to conquer Canaan; *"Have I not commanded you? Be strong and courageous. Do not be afraid; do not be discouraged, for the Lord your God will be with you wherever you go"* (Joshua 1:9 NIV). Let this be your anthem as you go all-in with God's plans for your life.

CHAPTER 2
All-In:
Fear of Inadequacy

When did we start believing that God wants to send us to safe places to do easy things?

That faithfulness is holding the fort? That playing it safe, is safe? That there is any greater privilege than sacrifice? That radical is anything but normal? Jesus didn't die to keep us safe.

He died to make us dangerous. ~ Mark Batterson

ONE MONTH AFTER my eye-opening mission trip in 2003, I proudly walked the stage at UCSB armed with a double major in Communications and Spanish, and a minor in Latin American Studies. Two months later, I found myself in Mexico, ready to immerse myself in the very orphanage that had stirred my soul just weeks prior.

When I filled out my application to serve, my commitment was resolute—one year doing anything needed. I envisioned utilizing my Spanish language and administrative skills, perhaps as a translator or in an office role. However, the unexpected awaited—a request for me to be a "house mom" for a group of boys aged one to ten, a total of seven energetic boys.

A mom?

Me?

A mom of seven?

A boy mom?

The party girl, fresh out of college?

Me?

Being a mom is a twenty four hour job, but being a mom to

seven is more than full-time. Truthfully, at this point in my life I didn't even like kids. Since swearing off marriage and children after my parents' tumultuous divorce, the prospect of being a mom to seven little boys was daunting. I was scared, unqualified, unprepared, and certainly, not enough.

Zig Ziglar once said that fear has two meanings: "Fear Everything And Run" or "Fear Everything and Rise."

The temptation to run back to comfort tugged at me. I felt akin to the Israelites, yearning to return to Egypt after Moses courageously confronted Pharaoh and led them out of oppression. I longed for the familiar, even if it meant returning to bondage and bypassing the desert's refining process.

> Yes, again, I said yes, even though I was afraid.

Motherhood was not in my plans, especially not for seven boys. However, my commitment to Jesus and my willingness to go all-in needed to outweigh my fears of inadequacy.

I had to rise.

Running was tempting, but I couldn't succumb. All-in, Jesus had said. So, with cold feet, I embraced motherhood. Yes, again, I said yes, even though I was afraid.

There it was. I gave my next yes to Jesus. I became a mom—a mom of seven. Because God has not given me a spirit of fear.

I clung to the words of David in Psalm 56:3-4 NLT:

But when I am afraid,
I will put my trust in you.
I praise God for what he has promised.
I trust in God, so why should I be afraid?
What can mere mortals do to me?

Navigating the Night—Lessons in the Refining Fire

My inaugural night in "Casa 6," aptly named "The Little Boy's House," unfolded as a riveting . . . let's call it . . . adventure.

Tasked with ensuring the well-being of seven little boys, the irony wasn't lost on me—I, who thought I would be working in a high-rise building in Los Angeles, was now living on the dirt roads of Mexico, taking care of children. Outwardly, I was confident, but inwardly I wrestled with insecurities and inadequacy. I found myself in a role I never anticipated.

This orphanage operated off the grid, powered by a generator that shut down at 10 p.m., leaving me with a flashlight as my sole source of light. The year was 2003, a time when cell phones were rudimentary, with games like the infamous Snake. With no electricity, providing adequate lighting required some ingenuity.

Managing bath time for seven energetic boys was a two-hour escapade, complete with water spillage, laughter, and my feeble attempts at figuring out "mom things." Post-bath rituals included dressing in PJs, brushing 140 teeth, saying seven goodnight prayers, and eventually getting them all into bed, and turning off the lights.

"I did it," I whispered in self-congratulation. Everyone was tucked into bed, including myself. Praise Jesus!

As I lay down, a grateful heart and a smile accompanied my thoughts. "I think I can do this," I told myself. The generator ceased, the desert heat pressed in, and sleep was elusive. No air conditioning and a motionless ceiling fan left me questioning how to survive the stifling heat. I promised myself a battery-operated camping fan from across the border on my next day off.

Suddenly, my oldest boy, Andres*[1], changed the night's trajectory. He yelled for me and began vomiting all over his room, in the pitch black of the night.

It was my first night as their house mom, and the generator was turned off. There was no electricity.

In a scramble, I searched for the flashlight my mom had given me. I tended to Andres, struggling to get him to the bathroom. Sitting in the pitch-black room with a faint yellow glow barely illuminating a square foot, I cleaned up vomit with my flashlight, feeling the weight of my new responsibility.

Looking heavenward, I questioned, "God, are you sure you called me?"

Silence.

I cried, scrubbed, sweated, and sobbed. What had I signed up for with this yes to Jesus? I wasn't cut out for this. Countless others, more qualified and less scared, could do a better job.

Yet, I was no quitter. Challenges fueled me. Unfortunately, this commitment proved the ultimate test.

That year at the orphanage was my time in the refining fire. Have you ever been put to the test, endured the process, and emerged stronger? Sometimes God raises the temperature in our lives, challenging and testing us and our faith.

> I cried, scrubbed, sweated, and sobbed. What had I signed up for with this yes to Jesus?

The Prophet Malachi speaks of this refiner's fire as he exhorts the people of Israel, telling them that the Lord will return and purify the nation with Holy Judgement.

But who can endure the day of his coming? Who can stand when he appears? He will be like a refiner's fire or a launderer's soap. He will sit as a refiner and purifier of silver; he will purify the Levites and refine them like gold and silver. Then the Lord will have men who will bring offerings in righteousness, and the offerings of Judah and Jerusalem will be acceptable to the Lord, as in days gone by, as in former years. ~ Malachi 3:2-4 NIV

The Prophet Isaiah also referred to the refiner's fire:

Behold, I have refined you, but not as silver; I have tested you
in the furnace of affliction. ~ Isaiah 48:10 NASB

The refiner's fire melts metals like gold or silver to purify them, removing impurities that surface as dross. This process continues until the refiner sees his own reflection in the metal.

Likewise, when we face affliction or hardship, God refines us to make us more like Him. The temporary difficulties mold our character, preparing us to accept Jesus' will—consistently. The refining fire can be painful, but God intends it to make us holy. The temporary afflictions are just that—momentary. The end product is increased trust, added faith, and diminished fear.

That first year working at the orphanage, I faced the fire repeatedly. Despite difficulties, tests, and trials, I fell in love with Jesus. He met me at every turn. I also fell in love with my boys and the other children. God performed open heart surgery on me, confronting my sins, attitudes, and apprehensions. Through prayer and Bible study, I shed my past and sinful ways, falling more in love with Jesus each day.

After that, there was no turning back. I was all-in, fully committed for the long journey ahead with the Lord, wherever He would lead me.

We Are All Called

Often, we elevate missionaries to a pedestal, seeing them as individuals we could never emulate. Who comes to mind when you think of someone truly ALL-IN for the Lord? Is it Mother Teresa, fearlessly serving in a leper colony; perhaps Heidi Baker, navigating through famine, plague, violence, and witchcraft in Mozambique, Africa; maybe Billy Graham, the influential American evangelist, or even Daniel in the lion's den, risking his life for his convictions? It might be your pastor or your hardworking mom who's doing whatever it takes for your success. These are ALL-IN types of people.

When God prompted me to go all-in on that first mission trip in June 2003, little did I know how those two words would echo through my journey of continually saying Yes to Jesus. I'm nowhere near the stature of Mother Teresa, Heidi Baker, Billy Graham, or Daniel. I'm an ordinary woman, grappling with fears and worries. Still, my desire is to fulfill God's will above all else, regardless of the cost or destination.

If God called this "party girl" to follow Him and go all-in with His plans and purposes, imagine what He could do with your yes. We are called to go all-in with His plans for our lives, despite our past, our present, or our sins. Your yes to Jesus may look different than mine. But your yes is just as important. We are all part of one body in Christ, and when we do our part, we will reach people. We will feed the poor, rescue the orphans, hold babies, cook dinners, and complete homework. We get to be Christ's hands and feet, reaching our family, friends, neighbors, and co-workers wherever God has us. You don't have to move to a foreign country to be a missionary. We are all missionaries when we make Jesus' last commandment our first priority (Mark 16:15). Wherever you are, wherever you work, that is your mission field. We are all called to do something for His kingdom. So, we all can go all-in with God's plans and purposes for our lives.

> We are called to go all-in with His plans for our lives, despite our past, our present, or our sins.

Christine Caine, the founder of A21 and Propel, said this one day on her social media:

> *Jesus is calling you to an all-in life.*
> *Being all-in isn't just for missionaries, martyrs,*
> *pastors, and church leaders.*
> *It's for you. For your family. For your kids. For your friends.*
> *Everyone is called to an all-in kind of faith*
> *that holds nothing back from God.*

Despite worries and doubts about your worthiness, uncertainties about God's will, regret over past mistakes, and fears of not discovering your purpose, you have the choice to embrace Jesus today. Say yes to Him, go all-in with His plans and commit wholeheartedly to wherever and however He is leading you.

Remember these words of the Apostle Paul:

But my life is worth nothing to me unless I use it for finishing the work assigned me by the Lord Jesus—the work of telling others the Good News about the wonderful grace of God. ~ Acts 20:24, NLT

> Let's take our feet out of the world, pursuing our selfish wants and needs, and let's leap in with both feet and follow Jesus.

Your purpose is to finish your assignment and the ministry that Jesus has given you. Maybe it's being a mom, a nurse, an accountant, a lawyer, an entrepreneur, a preacher, a pastor, or even a missionary. Whatever your calling is, let's go ALL-IN with His purpose for our lives, knowing that our life has no value other than completing the call God has for each of us, and testifying of God's amazing grace.

Let's take our feet out of the world, pursuing our selfish wants and needs, and let's leap in with both feet and follow Jesus. We are all called to live an all-in kind of life.

Chapter 3
Are You Willing?
The Power to Rise Above Fear

How very little can be done under the spirit of fear.
~ Florence Nightingale

IN THE DEPTHS OF DARKNESS, fear loomed over me like an unrelenting shadow, threatening to consume every inch of my being. Its chilling grip tightened around my heart, paralyzing me with doubt and uncertainty. But in that moment of despair, a flicker of courage emerged from the depths of my soul. With each step I took as I went all-in with God's plans and purposes, pushing past the boundaries of my comfort, I embraced the unknown, defying fear's grasp. In that defiance, I discovered the true essence of resilience—the power to rise above fear and transform it into unwavering strength. However, I still didn't feel brave.

Courage and wholehearted commitment are inseparable companions. The truth is that fear is an integral part of bravery. It may seem contradictory to merge these two words, but it holds true. Every valiant soul has been frightened on his or her journey of obeying God. Likewise, those who embrace God's purpose for their lives often wrestle with anxiety and must conquer it. I can personally attest to this. Frequently, we desire a complete understanding of God's plan or His ultimate destination for us before we say yes to His calling. Perhaps you find yourself in that very position. In my two decades of serving the Lord, in Mexico, I have come to realize that He typically reveals His will to us one step at a time, and it is our responsibility to trust the outcome to Him.

Are You Willing?

There is an Old Testament woman who was an all-in kind of person. An ordinary woman who said *yes* to God without knowing the outcome of her story. We find her in Genesis 24.

Abraham was now very old, and the Lord had blessed him in every way. He said to the senior servant in his household, the one in charge of all that he had, "Put your hand under my thigh. I want you to swear by the Lord, the God of heaven and the God of earth, that you will not get a wife for my son from the daughters of the Canaanites, among whom I am living, but will go to my country and my own relatives and get a wife for my son Isaac."

The servant asked him, "What if the woman is unwilling to come back with me to this land? Shall I then take your son back to the country you came from?" ~ Genesis 24:1-5, NIV

Have you ever been entrusted with an important task where the outcome hinged on your decision? Alternatively, have you ever been assigned a significant responsibility, only for the decision-making power to lie in someone else's hands?

In this story we find Abraham already old and looking for a wife for his son, Isaac. In that time and culture, the parents chose wives for their children. Have you ever seen the reality show series, *Married at First Sight?* The series features three to five couples, paired up by relationship experts, who agree to marry when they first meet. This show is a modern-day version of Abraham's search for Isaac's wife. In our Bible story, Abraham sends his servant, Eliezer, to return to the land of Abraham's ancestors to choose a wife for his son Isaac—a woman who would never even see Isaac before they married. What a difficult task for Eliezer!

Eliezer says to Abraham in verse five:

What if the woman is unwilling to come with me to this land?

Eliezer knows that most women have a "mind of their own."

One day she may say "Yes,"and then immediately change her mind. Right?

However, the divine purpose of God was being meticulously crafted and planned. Yet, there was one critical obstacle. What if the pivotal player, the woman, lacked willingness and courage to fulfill God's will for her life?

I love how Pastor Jack Hanes writes about this in his book, *His Last Command Our First Priority.* He says the entire plan hinged upon her participation. She would become Isaac's wife and, in the future, Jacob's mother. David's lineage would trace back to her descendants and, ultimately, the Lord Jesus Himself would be born through her family line.

But what if she was unwilling?

What if she resisted?

What if she refused to leave her family?

What if she rejected the calling to fulfill her purpose and destiny?

"We all have freedom of choice, but we do not have freedom of consequences."

The fulfillment of God's purpose relies upon the hearts of those who willingly embrace it. Will you choose to follow Him? Will you choose to align yourself with His will? How will God's will be completed on earth? Jesus himself prayed for it, saying, "*Your will be done on earth as it is in heaven*" (Matthew 6:10 NIV).

You might wonder how God's will actually comes to pass. It is accomplished through individuals who are willing—who wholeheartedly commit themselves to embracing His plans and purposes, who consciously choose to be obedient to His voice, even when fear tries to hold them back.

Many of us struggle to discern God's will in our lives. I personally faced this challenge until I stepped out of my comfort zone, embarked on a mission trip to Mexico, and heard God's voice resound clearly.

However, if you find yourself doubting God's will for your

own life, you can turn to the book of John and learn directly from Jesus. It is remarkable how you can seek answers to all your questions straight from God's Word.

For it is my Father's will that all who see his Son and believe in him should have eternal life. I will raise them up at the last day. ~ John 6:40, NLT

This is God's purpose for your life as well. It is God's will for ALL people to encounter Jesus, to place their faith in Him, and through that faith to obtain eternal life. As Jesus prepared to depart from this world after his resurrection, He entrusted His followers with a momentous command. In Mark 16:15 NIV, He proclaimed, "*Go into all the world and preach the gospel to all creation.*"

This commandment stands as Jesus's final instruction to His followers before ascending to heaven. Therefore, his last command must be our first priority.[1] It is our calling as believers.

YES in All Capital Letters

During my inaugural mission trip in 2003, God orchestrated a transformative experience that would forever alter the course of my life. Stepping outside my comfort zone, I attuned my ears to God's voice. It was on that day that God gave me a calling to join Him in the mission field—an unequivocal moment that would define my existence.

But what if I heard God's voice and found myself unwilling to comply? I acknowledged the freedom of choice I possessed, yet I also recognized the profound repercussions that would follow if I disregarded God's will for my life. Was I gripped by fear when it came to obeying God and going all-in? *YES*, in all capital letters! The future loomed before me, shrouded in uncertainty. I harbored apprehension about my past, questioning whether an ex-party girl like me could genuinely make a meaningful impact on a child's life.

Nevertheless, my greatest fear was being out of God's will, and not going all-in when He asked me to go. So, despite my fears, I said YES. I said YES to Jesus. YES to full-time ministry. YES, to leaving my old life. YES, to start a new one. YES to going ALL-IN with His plans even though I was scared.

I acknowledged the freedom of choice I possessed, yet I also recognized the profound repercussions that would follow if I disregarded God's will for my life.

Poverty Orphan

In that first year on the mission field, a remarkable encounter awaited me—I crossed paths with my now-husband, Daniel. Uniquely, he had grown up in the very orphanage we served, and when he reached the age of eighteen, he made the heartfelt decision to remain there and contribute to the ministry that had given him so much. He joined the staff and became an integral part of the team. Consequently, both of us found ourselves laboring at the orphanage when our paths intertwined.

My husband's background is that of a poverty orphan. His parents struggled to provide for him and his six siblings and, burdened by the weight of caring for their family, they would leave them home alone to find work. Consequently, their children were confined to their home—a mere 10'x10' shack—while his parents sought work opportunities. Given the absence of a daycare system in many parts of Mexico, mothers are left with the difficult choice of either staying at home or locking their children inside while they pursue employment. Tragically, some resort to the heart-wrenching decision of leaving their children at orphanages and relinquishing their parental rights. In the case of my husband's family, they opted to leave the children home alone, to fend for themselves.

One particularly vivid memory etched in his mind involves his youngest brother, Victor, who was just a few months old at the time. Victor would cry out for a bottle, but there was no milk to provide. However, they did have a well situated in their backyard. Lowering the bucket down, they would retrieve water, pour it into his bottle, add a pinch of sugar, and offer it to him in order to sustain his fragile existence.

Daniel can recall everyone huddling together on the floor in the confines of their one-room shack, which served as their collective sleeping quarters. He also recollects venturing out at the tender age of four or five, knocking on their neighbors' doors, and begging them for food. There were occasions when his parents would be absent for days or even weeks, desperately seeking employment to support their family.

On one fateful day, Daniel and his brother Chevo ventured to the train tracks near their humble home for a playful excursion. As they immersed themselves in their innocent amusement, they caught sight of a pair of police officers fixating their gaze upon them. It was evident that their bare feet, soiled appearance, and absence from school had not gone unnoticed. A sense of trepidation washed over Daniel and Chevo as they exchanged a knowing glance, fully aware that trouble was looming. They commenced their journey homeward, trailed closely by the police officers.

Upon reaching their house, the police officers posed the question of their parents' whereabouts. In response, the two young boys simply uttered, "They are working." The officers departed, momentarily allaying their concerns. However, a few hours later, the officers returned, armed with plywood. Determinedly, they nailed the plywood over the windows and doors, effectively sealing off any means of escape for the children. Furthermore, they declared their plans to revisit the following day, intent on confirming the presence of their parents. (You may find it perplexing how the police could take such actions. Nevertheless, it is important to bear in mind that Mexico is a third world country, where unconventional approaches are often employed.)

At daybreak, the police returned, eager to know whether the parents had made their appearance. Sadly, the anticipated reunion did not materialize, prompting the authorities to take Daniel and his siblings to the local police station. With no suitable arrangement in place to accommodate them, the officers temporarily confined them in a jail cell, the cold, unyielding bars serving as a stark reminder of their predicament. Despite the grim circumstances, Daniel reminisces about finding solace in the fact that the authorities provided them with warm and yummy food during their stay.

The following day, an organization known as DIF (The National System for Integral Family Development) came to their aid. DIF, akin to Child Protective Services in the United States, is a Mexican public institution dedicated to strengthening and promoting the well-being of families across the nation. Among its responsibilities is the placement of children in orphanages, as Mexico lacks a foster care system.

After being retrieved from the police station, they were transported to a Catholic orphanage in Tecate, B.C., Mexico. As a united family of siblings, they resided there for several months. Although visits from parents were permitted on weekends, Daniel's parents had yet to materialize. Subsequently, they were relocated from that orphanage to another, and then to yet another, until they eventually arrived at Rancho de Sus Niños, the orphanage they would call home. Unfortunately, his sisters were separated from the brothers during the many moves, and Daniel is unsure what happened to them.

Rancho de Sus Niños, was a Christian orphanage that not only instilled in them strong moral values but also nurtured a profound love for Jesus. At the tender age of eight, Daniel distinctly remembers embracing Jesus Christ as his Lord and Savior. Guiding him through the salvation prayer was his house mom, Julie, who relied on a translator as she spoke only English while Daniel spoke Spanish. Daniel shares that upon uttering that prayer, a profound transformation took place within him. Although he didn't outwardly exhibit excitement, a sense of peace resonated deep within. He shares, "I didn't feel the need to leap with joy, but deep within, I discovered peace. Regardless of what may lay ahead, I knew God would be by my side." Daniel and his brothers spent their formative years at this orphanage.

During my initial mission trip, I had the privilege of meeting Daniel. He was entrusted with overseeing our group's concrete project, and I distinctly remember engaging in conversations with him to practice my Spanish. Little did I know that God had plans in store for both of us—plans that would lead us to work together at the very same orphanage and eventually become husband and wife.

As I served at the orphanage as a house mom, God began the process of healing me from my past and my fears. It was during this time that I sensed God's prompting to pray for my future husband. Initially resistant, I voiced my concerns to God, stating that marriage was not my focus as I was committed to serving Him. However, God persistently urged me to pray for my yet-to-be-revealed spouse. Reluctantly, I surrendered and began praying for this unknown man. Once I wrapped my head around praying for a future husband, God later told me, "Start praying for Daniel." "But God," I said, "he is younger than me. He grew up in an orphanage, and we come from two totally different backgrounds. Are you sure?"

"Pray for Daniel," He repeated.

So, I was obedient and started praying for him. Little did I know, he was praying for me, too.

As my one-year commitment drew to a close, an undeniable

conviction arose within me signaling that I couldn't simply depart and return to my previous home. Deep in my heart, I sensed that Mexico had become my forever home. I kept my decision to myself, and Daniel remained unaware of my intention to extend my stay. He assumed that I might be preparing to leave. Unbeknownst to him, this realization prompted him to take a leap of faith.

Daniel and I shared a close friendship, often engaging in spirited basketball matches on the "cancha" (court) with the boys under my care. Through fervent prayer, I discovered an indescribable affection growing within me for him. It was through the sacred act of praying that I fell in love with him, yet I chose to remain silent, yearning for God to script our story according to His divine plan.

One evening, as I concluded bathing the boys I cared for, helping them brush their teeth, and offering bedtime prayers, a sudden knock echoed through my door. Dressed in my college sweatshirt emblazoned with the letters UCSB, adorned with water droplets from the bathing process, my hair tied up in a tired ponytail, I wearily opened the door, completely unaware of Daniel's presence. Given the strict regulations within the ministry, the opposite sex was prohibited from entering my house. Thus, we found ourselves standing on the porch, and our conversation unfolding within the confines of those external boundaries.

I couldn't help but notice Daniel's unmistakable nervousness. His gaze avoided meeting mine, his words faltered, and sweat droplets formed on his temple. Uncertainty enveloped me as his unease began to affect my own composure, amplifying the tension between us.

He said, "Heidi, I need to talk to you and tell you something." Then he was quiet and pensive. I didn't know what to say or what to do. I looked at my feet. It was silent for several minutes. His hands were sweating. He was physically nervous. Then, after several minutes, he looked up, looked into my eyes, and said, "Heidi, I don't know how to tell you this. But I have been praying for you, and God has told me a lot of things." I looked straight at him, my eyes as big as an owl's. I said to myself, "Is this really happening? Is this it?" I don't know what "it" was, but I thought it was happening.

Daniel proceeded and said, "I need to tell you something." And then there was a long pause. Then he blurted out, "I want to know if you will be my girlfriend, but I know you will be my wife." It was out. He said it. He unleashed his bravery with his surprising words. I wonder if I would recommend this bold strategy to all you single guys out there. But at that moment, I knew it was it. I knew my prayers for my future husband were being answered right before me. I looked at his deep brown, almost onyx eyes and said, "Yes, I know that too," with a giant smile. We embraced and laughed, and all the nervous tension changed to a giddy glee.

After committing to another year at Rancho de Sus Niños, I transitioned from being a house mom to an office assistant. This shift in roles granted me a fresh vantage point and revealed a new perspective on the inner workings of the orphanage system.

Mothers would come to the orphanage office and would ask to speak to the directors. Some would voluntarily drop off their kids because they couldn't put food on their tables or send them to school with a uniform and a backpack. However, one particular day stands out in my memory when a grandmother arrived, her tears flowing as she entrusted her three grandchildren to the orphanage. Overwhelmed by the heart-wrenching scene, I cried out to God, pleading for a solution. "God, there has to be another way. How can we keep these families together? How can we prevent the abandonment of children to orphanages and to the streets?"

A Holy Justice

That day marked a turning point in my life. It unveiled the darker side of orphan care, where parents resorted to using orphanages as temporary solutions, but, sadly, never returned for their children. The weight of this reality brought tears streaming down my face, stirring within me a profound sense of righteous indignation.

The truth is that a staggering eighty percent of children residing in orphanages still have living parents.[2] However, these parents are often trapped in the grips of poverty, unable to provide adequate care for their little ones. Compounding the issue is the absence of a daycare system in rural parts of Mexico, further exacerbating the challenges faced by families striving to stay together.

Recollections of the boys in my care surfaced in my mind, their longing to be reunited with their mothers echoing in my ears. Daniel, too, would share his own experiences of feeling abandoned, alone, and unloved during his time at the orphanage. It became painfully clear that if a reliable child-care system existed, these children would not have been subjected to the emotional toll of abandonment but would be forging a path towards a different narrative—one filled with love, family bonds, and belonging.

A few weeks later, Daniel and I came across a heart-wrenching newspaper article detailing the tragic fate of two young girls. Their parents, desperate to make ends meet, had locked them inside their home in Tijuana, while they went to work. In a devastating turn of events, a fire engulfed their home, claiming the lives of their innocent daughters.

Justice for these families blazed inside me like flames rising with the wind. The weight of these stories fueled an unyielding passion for justice within Daniel as well. As we constantly prayed for guidance regarding our marriage and the path God intended for us, these narratives continued to resurface with unwavering persistence. It was as if they formed a piercing bullseye on our hearts. The question echoed relentlessly: Why don't we start our own non-profit organization and fight to keep families together?

My husband intimately understands the profound damage that

ensues when parents leave their children home alone, also the deep sentiments of growing up in an orphanage. Furthermore, I had personally witnessed families surrendering their parental rights to these institutions under the false belief that it would offer their children "a better life." These experiences crystallized our resolve. We would embark on a mission to create a no-cost childcare facility, ensuring no child would ever be locked in their homes while their parents were at work or sent to an orphanage due to poverty, in the communities God called us to serve.

With unwavering determination, we set out to build an organization that would champion the cause of family preservation, sparing no effort to ensure that every child receives the love, care, and opportunities he or she deserves within the embrace of their own families.

So, once we were married, we started our organization called Open Arms Childcare Ministries, where we fight to keep families together by providing a faith-based children's center for the most vulnerable children. We took the name from a passage in Mark, where Jesus was ministering to the children:

People were bringing little children to Jesus for him to place his hands on them, but the disciples rebuked them. When Jesus saw this, he was indignant. He said to them, "Let the little children come to me, and do not hinder them, for the kingdom of God belongs to such as these. Truly I tell you, anyone, who will not receive the kingdom of God like a little child will never enter it." And he <u>took the children in his arms</u>, placed *his hands on them and blessed them.* (Emphasis mine.) ~ Mark 10:13-16 NIV

Inspired by the boundless love of Jesus for children and fueled by the desire to prevent the plight of orphans, we yearned to open our arms and provide a safe haven for the children of Mexico. Our vision was to embrace them within our care during the day, while working diligently to avert the tragedy of parent-child separation.

Drawing inspiration from the biblical account of Nehemiah's unwavering commitment to rebuilding the walls of Jerusalem, despite formidable opposition, we resolved to stand firm in defense of families. Like Nehemiah, we adopted a proactive stance, determined to safeguard the unity and well-being of families in our community.

After I looked things over, I stood up and said to the nobles, the officials, and the rest of the people, "Don't be afraid of them. Remember the Lord, who is great and awesome, and fight for your families, your sons and your daughters, your wives and your homes. (Emphasis mine.) ~ Nehemiah 4:14 NIV

"Fight for Families" has become our slogan. However, when you put a poor missionary girl and an orphan boy together, you basically get *zero.* We had nothing but love, and a vision from God. Inevitably, we found ourselves in a situation where we literally had one dollar in our pocket. Following our marriage in August of 2005, my mother and stepfather graciously purchased a house for us, complete with an adjacent plot of land. This generous gift provided us with the ideal setting to establish a small childcare facility to serve the underprivileged families in the village of La Misión. Nestled between Rosarito and Ensenada, approximately an hour south of the San Diego border, La Misión became the focal point of our ministry.

Armed with determination and faith, we embarked on fundraising efforts and diligently spread the word about our mission. We sent newsletters to the one hundred and fifty individuals on our wedding list, fervently praying and firmly believing that God would provide for the needs of this ministry. But, let's just say, it was rough getting started.

The $1

Now, I am not exaggerating. We literally got to a point where we had one dollar to our names. We couldn't proceed. We couldn't even eat. I was so petrified at this point that we would never have enough. I was afraid we might not have heard God's voice correctly and we were out of His will. My worst-case scenario became my reality at that moment. We had nothing except for ONE DOLLAR. My old fears started creeping in, like insidious shadows lurking in the corners of my mind. They slithered through the corridors of my thoughts, silently weaving their web of doubt and uncertainty, threatening to entangle me in their suffocating embrace. Like nocturnal creatures emerging from their hiding places, these fears prowled within me, ready to pounce at the slightest hint of vulnerability, and I began to doubt whether we had heard God's voice.

I clearly remember the day when a wrong turn brought us to the one dollar situation. We had to drive to Rosarito to pay our electric bill. (People still had to stand in line and pay in cash back in 2005.) I remember that we accidentally got on the toll road on the way back home. We had meant to take the libre (free) road, but we missed the turn. We pulled up to the toll road, and I handed Daniel two dollars to pay the toll, and I sat there silently with one dollar left in my hand. Finally, I looked at him and said, "Daniel, we only have one dollar to our name. We can't even care for ourselves; how are we supposed to build a daycare center and save the world." The thirty-minute ride home was silent as we sat contemplating our next steps.

We got home, felt defeated, and entertained feelings of fear, but I refused to succumb to their haunting presence. I stood tall, like a vigilant lighthouse amidst a stormy sea, casting my beacon of hope and resilience into the darkness. With each passing wave of fear, I fortified my inner sanctuary, building walls of courage and determination to shield myself from their relentless assault.

> I plucked each fear from the fertile soil of my mind. I nurtured the seeds of faith,...

Just as a gardener tends to a blooming oasis, diligently uprooting the weeds that threaten to overshadow the vibrant blossoms, I plucked each fear from the fertile soil of my mind. I nurtured the seeds of faith, watering them with the unwavering trust that if God had called us to this, He would provide, and like a phoenix rising from the ashes, my spirit soared above the smothering grip of those old fears. I unleashed my bravery in this moment, embraced the winds of change, spread my wings of resilience and soared towards the limitless sky of possibility. For within me, a newfound strength had taken root, transforming those creeping fears into stepping-stones on the path to personal growth and triumph.

> ...if God had called us to this, He would provide,...

That night, we got on our knees and held our last dollar up to heaven. We said, "God, here is our last dollar. We give you all we have. We give you our dream of fighting for families. We know that your heartbeat is to keep families together. God, we are ALL-IN, but we can't do it alone. We need a sign that you are with us, and if you have called us to this, we know you will provide."

The following day, we woke up. I had to push away all fear and arise full of faith. To tell you the truth. There was a pain in the pit of my stomach. I recognized it right away—worry. We took a walk in the local park and ran into an American couple. We started talking to them and told them about what we were doing and why we were there in Mexico. They were a Christian couple on a mission trip at the local orphanage. We asked if they wanted to come to check out our property and see the vision of our ministry and they said, "Yes." We gave them a quick tour of our new home, a soon-to-be renovated childcare center where children ran the halls giggling. They definitely had to use their imagination to see it, but before they left, they wrote us a check for two hundred and fifty dollars. Now, when you have one dollar in your pocket, two hundred and fifty dollars feels like an astronomical amount of money. That was the unmistakable sign that we needed. We knew that God had answered our prayers. My faith grew, and my fear dissipated. He was Jehovah Jireh—My Provider—who shall I fear?

Ever since the day we gave that last dollar back to God, He has shown up every step of the way. Isaiah 58:11 says; *"Where God guides, He provides."* You need to hear that, too, today. Where God guides you, if it is His will, He will provide for you.

God would not put a dream in my heart if he didn't give me everything I needed to fulfill it. That goes for you, also. If God has put a desire on your heart, He will provide you with everything you need to accomplish it, but you must believe and follow Him, even if you are scared.

If anyone has believed in God and his promises *over and over and over* again, it is me. If I am going to be really honest with you, believing God has not always been easy for me. It has been scary and is a lifelong journey. Sometimes I have been fearful of trusting God. Believing He would provide for us when we had only one dollar truly stretched my faith.

People who believe in God have problems just like other people. What distinguishes someone who steps out in faith, even if they are scared, is what they do when faced with unbelief. How is God supposed to reveal His faithfulness unless we exercise our faith?

I learned that I couldn't move into all God had for me and become all He created me to be without surrendering my life, will, thoughts, FEARS, and even my last dol-

> How is God supposed to reveal His faithfulness unless we exercise our faith?

lar to the Lord. Ever since we got on our knees and prayed that prayer for provision, we have only seen God's blessing and support flow in our lives and ministry.

Twenty years ago, Open Arms was just a dream. Today, God has provided three beautiful campuses caring for hundreds of children, a teen center, a medical and dental clinic, and growing and active churches. We have seen miracle after miracle.

We have even rescued ten children from orphanages who were only there for financial reasons. They are now back with their parents and in our care during the day.

> God has taken two ordinary people and has done the extraordinary because we went ALL IN, despite our fears.

God has taken two ordinary people and has done the extraordinary because we went ALL IN, despite our fears. We are just two willing people—willing to do God's will.

How many children would be in orphanages?

How many children would be on the streets or locked in their homes while their parents are at work?

How many families wouldn't be together?

How many people wouldn't have had the opportunity to know Jesus?

How will others live, if we aren't willing to give or get a little

WE MAY NEVER TRULY COMPRE-
HEND THE MAGNITUDE OF EVERY
SACRIFICE MADE OR TOIL EN-
DURED DURING ARDUOUS AND
ENDLESS DAYS OR THE RELENTLESS
ASSAULTS ON OUR SPIRITS. YET,
AMIDST THE ENIGMA OF IT ALL,
THERE REMAINS AN UNWAVERING
TRUTH—WHEN WE WHOLE-
HEARTEDLY SAY YES TO HIM, THE
WORTH BECOMES IMMEASURABLE.

uncomfortable to follow Him, no matter what the cost?

We may never truly comprehend the magnitude of every sacrifice made or toil endured during arduous and endless days or the relentless assaults on our spirits. Yet, amidst the enigma of it all, there remains an unwavering truth—when we wholeheartedly say *yes* to Him, the worth becomes immeasurable.

Abraham's servant pondered, *"What if the woman is not willing?"*

What if her ears remain closed to the message?

What if she is consumed by her own desires?

What if she is fixated on her own ambitions?

What if she clings to the comfort of her own country, reluctant to step beyond its boundaries?

What if she hesitates to fully embrace the divine plan set before her?

Will God's message reach the lost and the broken?

Yet, in the midst of uncertainty, the servant's doubts and fears were met with a resounding truth. Though doubts may flicker like a fragile flame, the indomitable light of His purpose pierces through the shadows of hesitation.

For when the hearts of the willing align with the whispers of the divine, the transformative power of God's message resounds throughout the ages. It transcends the boundaries of ego, shatters the barriers of self-focus, and calls us to venture beyond our comfort zones. In the resolute surrender of a willing heart, the symphony of God's redemptive love resonates, reaching the depths of a lost and dying world.

So, let not the "what ifs" deter the faithful, nor the doubts extinguish the flame of hope. For in the tapestry of heaven, every thread of willingness, every note of obedience, every ounce of unleashed bravery, weaves a profound narrative that echoes across generations.

Within this grand tapestry, you hold an irreplaceable role! Your willingness to proclaim the good news becomes the very breath that animates its existence. For what significance lies in the sacrifice of Christ upon the cross if the world remains unaware? What power resonates in the words, "*God so loved the world that He gave His only Son,*" (John 3:16) if that message remains confined within the depths of our hearts?

For in the tapestry of heaven, every thread of willingness, every note of obedience, every ounce of unleashed bravery, weaves a profound narrative that echoes across generations.

By stepping out of your comfort zone and braving God's call, you have the power to make a difference in the lives of those who are lost and searching for hope. Each sacrifice, every challenging day, and every spiritual attack you face is worth it when you choose to say yes to Him.

But was the woman willing to leave her family and homeland and marry Isaac? This woman's name is Rebekah, and we see her response in Genesis 24: 54-58 NIV.

When they got up the next morning, he [Abrahams's servant] said, "Send me on my way to my master." But her brother and her mother replied, "Let the young woman remain with us ten days or so; then you may go. "But he said to them, "Do not detain me, now that the Lord has granted success to my journey. Send me on my way so I may go to my master. "Then they said, "Let's call the young woman and ask her about it." So they called Rebekah and asked her, "Will you go with this man?"

"I will go," she said.

She Was Willing! She Was Brave!

Because she was willing, the plan of God would not fail. Because she was willing, the purpose of God prevailed. Because she was willing to go, she would become a channel through which the Messiah would come to the world. Rebekah was an all-in type of woman.

Are You Willing?

The greatest thing you can do is to be willing to say *Yes* to the will of God, even if you are afraid.

Jesus did the will of his Father. He came to earth and died a brutal death on the cross because he loved you and me. He was ALL-IN, even unto death. Are you willing to leave your comfort zone and say yes to Jesus? Maybe you have already given your life to Him; are you willing to go deeper? Are you ready to go all-in with His plans and purposes for your life?

You are a vessel through which God's message of salvation can be delivered to a world that desperately needs it. The impact of Christ's sacrifice on the cross is magnified when it is shared with others. It is through your willingness to go, to proclaim the good news, and to live out His love that the transformative power of God's grace can reach the hearts of those who are perishing.

Don't underestimate the significance of your role in His plan. You have the opportunity to be a beacon of light, guiding others towards eternal life. Your obedience and commitment are essential to ensuring that the message of God's love and redemption is known and received by those who need it.

So, embrace your purpose and cling to the calling that God has placed upon your life. You can rise above fear when you are willing to do His will. Step forward with faith, knowing that your willingness to go and share His message is vital. The world is waiting for your yes.

God may not be asking you to give up everything and move to another country, but He is urging you to take that next step today. Will you give towards missions? Will you go on a mission trip? Will you cross the street and tell your neighbor about Jesus? Will you step up and serve in your church? Friends, are you willing?

Are you willing to take the next step to go all-in? He is waiting for you with open arms. Take one step at a time and be willing. *His plans are above and beyond anything you can ever think of or imagine* (Ephesians 3:20-21).

> You can rise above fear when you are willing to do His will.

I know God is speaking to your heart. I know God is stirring some of you in a new direction. I know God is telling you to believe Him. Believe Him for a miracle. Believe Him for a miraculous provision. Believe Him for every need. I am praying that God will give you the courage. That he would make you brave enough to step out and believe Him. Because being brave isn't the absence of fear; it is doing it anyway, even when you are scared.

So, don't wait for fear to disappear before taking action. Embrace the fear, acknowledge its presence, and let it fuel your determination to move forward. Understand that unleashing your bravery lies in taking that first step, even when your heart is pounding, and your mind is filled with doubt. Each act of courage strengthens your resilience, builds your character, and opens up new possibilities for growth.

Remember, being brave is not about being fearless; it's about being willing to confront your fears and take the necessary steps towards saying yes to Jesus. Be courageous, face your fears, and let your actions speak louder than your doubts. In doing so, you will discover a strength within that you never knew existed, and you will inspire others to be brave in their own journeys. I want to encourage you to be willing to

> Remember, being brave is not about being fearless; it's about being willing to confront your fears and take the necessary steps towards saying yes to Jesus.

do His will—constantly—even when you are afraid.

Was She Willing?

Going back to our story in Genesis 24. Just like Eliezer said to Abraham, *"What if the woman is not willing?"* I think about that too.

What if I was not willing to go?

What if I was not willing to leave my possessions behind, or leave a well-paying job and a college degree?

What if I didn't say *yes* to God's will and His plan for my life?

How many children would be in orphanages?

How many children would be on the streets or locked in their homes while their parents are at work?

How many families wouldn't be together?

How many people wouldn't have had the opportunity to know Jesus?

How will others live if we aren't willing to give or get a little uncomfortable to follow Him, no matter what the cost?

Everyone is called to an all-in kind of faith that holds nothing back from God.

Today, despite fears of inadequacy, anxieties about missing God's will, horror at disobedience, fear that your past disqualifies you, or apprehensions about never finding your purpose, you can say *Yes* to Jesus. You can go all-in wherever and however He's calling you.

> Everyone is called to an all-in kind of faith that holds nothing back from God.

Remember these words of the Apostle Paul:

But my life is worth nothing to me unless I use it for finishing the work assigned me by the Lord Jesus—the work of telling others the Good News about the wonderful grace of God. ~ Acts 20:24, NLT

Chapter 4
The God of the 11th Hour:
Fear That God Is Insufficient

Not that we are sufficient in ourselves to claim anything as coming from us, but our sufficiency is from God. ~ 2 Corinthians 3:5 ESV

HAVE YOU EVER FELT that your needs were too great for God? In Mexico, where the need is extravagant at times, there are moments when I find myself questioning whether God's provision is sufficient to meet the overwhelming number of needs. During times when our resources have dwindled to just one dollar, doubts crept in, causing me to question if I truly heard God's voice in the first place. However, the staggering statistics and heart-wrenching stories of children living in orphanages serve as a constant reminder that we must press on with our mission to build Open Arms, despite the scarcity we face, and despite the fear that creeps into our thoughts.

> ...perhaps one of the most devastating forms of poverty is growing up without the presence of a mother or a father.

When we think of Mexico or any other third-world country, our initial thoughts may revolve around poverty, drugs, or the plight of orphaned children. However, after spending two decades on the mission field, I want to share a different perspective. Most people we encounter simply want to be a family, desiring to be together regardless of their impoverished conditions—even if it means living in a humble one-bedroom shack with a dirt floor and no running water. The struggle for the family unit is real in these places, and perhaps one of the most devastating forms of poverty is growing up without the presence of a mother or a father.

Unfortunately, in Mexico and numerous other developing nations, there are limited options available for those in distress. The government lacks the abundant resources, comprehensive programs, and genuine care for the well-being of its people. RELAF (Red Latinoamericana de Acogimiento Familiar) reported that in Mexico alone a staggering 1,600,000 are considered "orphans". [1] However, it is essential to debunk the misconception that children residing in orphanages have necessarily lost one or both parents. In fact, the truth, as revealed by Save the Children, is that eighty to ninety percent of children living in an orphanage worldwide have at least one living parent.[2] These children are placed in orphanages due to poverty-related circumstances and are being raised by institutions rather than in the family structure that God designed. Abandonment by destitute families, unable to provide for all their children, is a common cause of this heartbreaking situation in Mexico.

By shedding light on the reality of orphan care, we can begin to comprehend the depth of the challenge before us. Our mission is not solely about meeting immediate needs but preventing children from going to orphanages just for poverty reasons.

During my time working at the orphanage in Mexico, I have witnessed heart-wrenching scenes of desperate mothers reluctantly leaving their children behind.

They are driven to make this complex and agonizing decision because they simply cannot afford to provide food, clothing, or basic school supplies. Their hope is to give their children a chance at a better life within the walls of an orphanage where they might have a roof over their heads, food in their bellies, and clothes on their backs. However, what these mothers may not realize is that the psychological trauma of abandonment often leads to even worse outcomes than enduring poverty within their own families.

As I read the startling studies of the devastating consequences of being abandoned, I am overwhelmed:

- An estimated eight million children live in orphanages and other institutions worldwide, but eighty percent are not orphans.
- Children who grow up in orphanages are at much higher risk of becoming victims of violence, trafficking and exploitation.[3]
- Research shows orphanages harm children's social, emotional, and cognitive development.
- Institutionalization of very young children has a similar impact on early brain development as severe malnutrition or maternal drug use during pregnancy
- Young adults raised in institutions are ten times more likely to fall into sex work than their peers, and 500 times more likely to take their own lives.
- Placing a child in an orphanage quadruples the risk of sexual violence.[4]
- A shocking statistic reveals that one out of every twenty children under the age of five is left home alone or under the care of another child under the age of ten. [5]

I have lived in an orphanage while serving these precious children. I have walked on the dirt roads. I see the hunger, poor hygiene, and poverty of these little ones. My heart is broken, and, at times, I am impatient because I can't do enough. I'm aware that children who grow up in institutions show cognitive and developmental delays, as well as decreased brain activity, and a greatly elevated incidence of psychiatric disorders. Children under the age of three are particularly vulnerable to the effects of institutionalization.[6] Depending on how long a child spends in an institution, the consequences can last a lifetime. I'm aware of the negative consequences—and even more so is our Lord. However, God has given us a vision and we see and hear their plight. It is my prayer that God will help others see the tragic dilemma that these children are experiencing.

I am personally blessed to have a wonderful husband who grew up in an orphanage and suffered much because of the abandonment. But someone—someone helped him, and he is a tremendous father, husband, and leader for Christ. I am a firm believer in the biblical mandate to protect and care for the "fatherless" and the "orphan." Psalm 82:3 NIV resonates deeply with me: "Defend the weak and the fatherless; uphold the cause of the poor and the oppressed.

True justice lies not only in caring for orphans after they have been abandoned or separated from their parents, but also in actively preventing such circumstances from occurring. In my opinion, prevention should be at the forefront of missional efforts, shining a brighter light and demanding just as much attention as orphan care. This is the essence of justice. This is defending the poor and the orphan. Let us defend the orphan before they become one! Yes, let us care for the orphans and children in orphanages without a doubt. But let us also fight tirelessly to ensure that no child becomes an orphan in the first place.

> Let us defend the orphan before they become one!

I encourage each of you, after hearing the story of my husband, hearing the stories first-hand of working at an orphanage, and seeing the dire statistics, that we, as the Body of Christ, rise up. Let's embrace courageous faith and say *yes* to Jesus by championing the cause of keeping families together, for it is in this pursuit that we reflect God's heart of love, restoration, and justice in a broken world.

I am not naive to the fact that some children must be removed from their homes due to death, disease, violence, abuse, or extreme neglect. However, children should never have to grow up in an orphanage solely because they are considered "poverty orphans." What if more people came alongside families and worked with the most vulnerable children in each community so poverty, violence, abuse, and neglect never become why a child grows up in an institution? Whether we consider foster care or orphanage care, it is clear that both systems have their flaws. Many foster moms have shared with me that the system may even hurt the child more than their own families did. Similarly, having visited numerous orphanages in Mexico, I have seen firsthand that only a few provide a truly healthy environment for children. Parents are imperfect, the system is flawed, and orphan care falls short. Thus, it is vital that we take a closer look at the prevention side of orphan care and seek true preservation of the family unit.

There are so many creative people in the Kingdom of God. I am praying that our Lord will give heavenly ideas for new programs and solutions to this heartbreaking reality. God is a God of miracles and will give divine thoughts to us and to you. Please pray with us. Please pray that we will have supernatural energy, creative ideas, and people who will partner with us. You might very well be one of the called ones.

Together, we can fight to keep children with their families and support organizations and individuals working tirelessly towards this cause. God has ordained the family, and it is our duty to give our all to work alongside families in the most vulnerable situations and to preserve the family unit. I am committed to finding solutions for the brokenness within families. I am dedicated to keeping families together and to preventing the abandonment of children. I am determined to be proactive in helping children stay with their families when they face the risk of going to an orphanage.

Fight for Families

I am grateful for the Christian orphanage and the loving people who nurtured my husband, and helped shape him into the person he is today. But it does not diminish the fact that he never knew if his parents loved him, wanted him, or would ever return for him. It doesn't erase the blood bond between him and his birth parents, even though they are ridden with poverty. It doesn't heal the hole in his heart that only his mother can fill. I am thankful that he found Jesus at the orphanage and that his basic needs were met. However, overcoming the orphan spirit can be a lifelong journey. We are grateful that my husband feels God's heartbeat and recognizes that families are part of God's divine plan. He also understands that his birth family lacked the resources and support of a ministry to come alongside them, offering the assistance and tools they needed to keep their family together. Healing has taken place because God is our ultimate healer. Yet, the fight continues. We fight by opening our arms to Mexico's most vulnerable children and families, working diligently to help them stay together.

Our mission is to provide support that allows families to stay united while offering children access to nutrition, education, psychological assistance, and biblical training, all without removing a child from his or her family. We strive to achieve this through the provision of no-cost childcare centers.

Many parents in the United States can empathize with the struggle of finding reliable childcare, but the situation becomes even more challenging for working parents in Mexico. In most Mexican households, both parents must work to make ends meet. Single mothers and single fathers have no choice but to seek employment outside the home. However, many parts of Mexico and Latin America still lack sufficient infrastructure to provide accessible public childcare options.

It is crucial to understand that without affordable care options, working parents often face the heartbreaking decision of either locking the children in their home while they go to work, where they are at risk of abuse, sex trafficking, burning their homes down, and so many other dangers of being home alone. Or voluntarily placing them in an orphanage. At Open Arms, we provide no-cost childcare services and strive to combat this problem by offering a safe haven during the day for children whose families need it most. Our assistance extends beyond basic childcare; we are not like your typical daycare center found in the United States.

Instead, we provide a nurturing home away from home, enabling children to grow up within their families. Our goal is to eliminate the need for mothers to leave their children unsupervised at home or consider giving them up to an orphanage.

To be honest, the fight to keep families together is a formidable one, and it is our collective responsibility to uphold justice for the poor and the orphan. Preventing the abandonment of children is an important way we can fulfill this duty.

When we embarked on our journey to establish Open Arms and prevent child abandonment, we faced numerous obstacles. With each obstacle, fear and worry would creep into my heart like a prowling lion, and I would question whether God would come through once again. Yet, time and time again, we experienced God's incredible provision. First, my mother's church reached out and informed us that they were sending a mission team to assist with construction and would provide the necessary finances for the project. Then, a friend informed us about someone willing to invest their inheritance, resulting in a generous donation of $20,000. Miracle after miracle unfolded before our eyes. God took us to the lowest point, down to having just one dollar, so that we could learn to trust Him when we had almost nothing. And every time we placed our trust in God and exercised our faith, our fears dissipated as we witnessed Him providing for all our needs.

In moments when fear stealthily entered my life like a thief in the night, I clung to the words of Psalm 34: 4-8 NIV:

I sought the Lord, and he answered me; he delivered me from all my fears.

Those who look to him are radiant; their faces are never covered with shame.

This poor man called, and the Lord heard him; he saved him out of all his troubles.

The angel of the Lord encamps around those who fear him, and he delivers them.

Taste and see that the Lord is good; blessed is the one who takes refuge in him.

As I learned to depend on the Lord to meet all our needs, including the needs of the children we served, He gradually eradicated all my fears. Every time we called upon Him, He rescued us from our problems, and He continues to do so. My fear that God would not be enough, that He would not provide, diminished as my fear of the Lord grew. I can genuinely testify that time and time again, I have tasted the goodness of the Lord and found refuge in Him. My desire was to create that same refuge for the children and families in Mexico. Together, with God as our provider and refuge, we can overcome fear, provide for the needs of vulnerable children, and work tirelessly to preserve the sanctity of the family unit.

> My fear that God would not be enough, that He would not provide, diminished as my fear of the Lord grew.

Our God Who Provides in the 11th Hour

Just before we were to receive our first visiting mission team to Baja, a significant hurdle stood in our way. The house we purchased for the childcare facility had electrical lines running directly above its roof. Our plan was to add a second story for us to live in, while the first floor would be remodeled to become the childcare facility. About six months prior to the team's arrival, I reached out to CFE, the electric utility company in Mexico, asking for them to send linemen to relocate the lines. It seemed like a straightforward fix, as having electrical lines directly above a home posed serious safety risks. However, I encountered countless obstacles and resistance. They instructed me to visit their offices and fill out a request, then they assured me they would "work on it." Little did I know what "working on it" meant in a third-world country. I followed their instructions and waited patiently for months, but nothing happened. Frustrated, I called the offices again, asking to speak with a supervisor, only to be abruptly hung up on. It was clear that customer service was not a priority for them. Livid with anger and frustration, I realized that I was afraid that God might not show up for us, and this was causing me to doubt God's sufficiency.

As the mission group's arrival drew near, the electrical lines still loomed over our roof. It seemed like we would have no choice but to cancel our first mission team. I feared that if we couldn't even get the electric company to relocate their lines after numerous attempts, no other group would be willing to schedule with us in the future. Finally, I turned to prayer. Regrettably, it wasn't my first course of action; I had initially treated Jesus as a 911 call, believing that simply submitting the correct paperwork would resolve the issue. But I was wrong, and I found myself in need of another miracle from Jesus. Would He come through for us again? Doubt and fear began to take hold of me.

In desperation, I approached God and said, "God, I cannot do this in my own strength. I have tried and failed. God, I need You to move these lines over our roof. You showed up when we had only one dollar. You have provided this mission team to help us build. Will You please intervene and relocate these lines?"

Honestly, I had no other option but to trust God. He had to make a way where there seemed to be no way, or else we would have to cancel the mission trip. Fear of not being able to continue grasped hold of me. I was in fight or flight mode.

I chose to fight. I chose to put my trust in Him and his sufficiency, even though it terrified me.

Just one week before the mission team was scheduled to serve, the entire town of La Misión experienced a power outage. Curious about the situation, I glanced out the window, hoping for some answers. To my amazement, I saw a lineman in a white bucket on his electrical truck, working on the post right next to our house. They were actually relocating the lines! It was a true eleventh-hour miracle. Once again, God had proven Himself faithful. This showed me that I could not only believe in God, but I could truly believe that He is who He says He is. Time and time again, He has shown me that I can trust Him as my provider, and I no longer have to worry about Him not showing up.

> This showed me that I could not only believe in God, but I could truly believe that He is who He says He is.

The eleventh hour means *the absolute latest time before it is too late.* It is a phrase that means "at the last moment" and is found in Matthew 20: 1-16 where Jesus taught the Parable o f Workers in the Vineyard.

In this parable, a landowner went out early in the day to hire workers to tend the vineyard and settled on paying them a denarius a day. At the third hour of the day, he went out and saw others unproductive, so he hired them also. At the sixth and ninth hours, he went again and saw other workers standing around, so he hired them also. Finally, at the eleventh hour, he found others standing idle. Let's look at Matthew 20: 6-7 NIV:

About five in the afternoon, he saw others standing around. He asked them, "Why have you been standing here all day long doing nothing?" "Because no one has hired us," they answered. He said to them, "You also go and work in my vineyard."

At the end of the day, the landowner paid every worker a denarius, as was agreed upon with the first set of workers who started early in the morning. In other words, the workers hired at the eleventh hour worked for only one hour but still received the same amount as those who worked all day. That is God's grace at work!

You receive the eleventh-hour miracle when it seems like time is running out. It appears that God won't come through. God is still in the business of providing eleventh-hour miracles. Whatever you are going through or need, God can activate the eleventh-hour miracle.

Jesus calls us to shift our perspective from the natural things and seek His Kingdom. He is not just saying, *Hey you, stop worrying.* No, he is saying, *It is all in your perspective.* Instead of worrying about the day-to-day things, He asks us to stop fretting and put our energy into what is really important, His Kingdom and His righteousness.

But seek first his kingdom and his righteousness, and all these things will be given to you as well. Therefore, do not worry about tomorrow, for tomorrow will worry about itself. Each day has enough trouble of its own. ~ Mathew 6:33-34 NIV

Our job is to seek Him. He wants to provide. It's His character. Why did I ever doubt?

Have you ever doubted that God would come through for you? Have you ever worried that He wouldn't provide for you? I just want to remind you of the goodness of our God. He has your best interests at heart. He loves you and will care for you. Sometimes we have to trust, and yes, even in the eleventh hour. That is when our faith is truly put to the test.

Are you waiting on God to move? Are you waiting on Him to provide? Are you trusting His timing? God's timing is not always our timing, but His timing is always

> God's timing is not always our timing, but His timing is always perfect.

perfect. God is never late. Trust Him, and remember He is calling you to big things, to go all-in with His plans and purposes. Don't hesitate to say Yes even when you are scared. God always shows up. Your prayers can activate the eleventh-hour miracle.

Four ways to experience an eleventh-hour miracle: These are practical steps that have made a significant impact in my own life and journey.

1. Worship and Rejoice: Let's turn to Paul's letter to the Thessalonians. Paul gives us some practical pointers in this letter as he prepares the Thessalonians for the day of the Lord. Then, after he readies them for Jesus's return, he speaks to them about their personal worship, which I genuinely believe can usher in the eleventh-hour miracle.

Rejoice always, pray continually, give thanks in all circumstances; for this is God's will for you in Christ Jesus. Do not quench the Spirit. ~ 1 Thessalonians 5:16-19 NIV

Rejoicing is always a powerful weapon. Even in the midst of challenging times, we have the choice to rejoice and praise God. It moves the heart of God and invites His presence into our lives. As Paul reminds us in Philippians 4:4-8 NIV, *Rejoice in the Lord always. I will say it again: Rejoice! Let your gentleness be evident to all. The Lord is near. Do not be anxious about anything, but in every situation, by prayer and petition, with thanksgiving, present your requests to God. And the peace of God, which transcends all understanding, will guard your hearts and your minds in Christ Jesus.*

2. Pray Continually and Give Thanks: These are essential aspects of our relationship with God. Prayer is simply our way of communicating with Him, and we can engage in it anywhere and at any time. Let's remember the words of Jesus in Mark 11:24 NIV, where He says, *Therefore I tell you, whatever you ask for in prayer, believe that you have received it, and it will be yours.* Prayer is not a last resort or a 911 call; it is an ongoing conversation with our Heavenly Father.

Giving thanks in all circumstances opens the gates of heaven. Cultivating an attitude of gratitude shifts our perspective and acknowledges our reliance on God. When we recognize that we can do nothing without Him, we position ourselves to experience His provision and intervention. As Isaiah 12:4-5 NLT reminds us, *On that wonderful day, you will sing: 'Thank the Lord! Praise His name! Tell the nations what He has done. Let them know how mighty He is! Sing to the Lord, for He has done wonderful things. Make known His praise around the world.'*

3. Do not quench the Spirit: 1 Thessalonians 5:19 is a powerful reminder to depend on the Holy Spirit in all aspects of life and ministry. We hinder His work when we rely on our own strength or methods. Whether it is creating hope, maintaining joy, or carrying out good works, we must rely on the power of the Spirit. As we read in Romans 15:13 NIV, *"May the God of hope fill you with all joy and peace as you trust in Him so that you may overflow with hope by the power of the Holy Spirit."*

> Whether it is creating hope, maintaining joy, or carrying out good works, we must rely on the power of the Spirit.

4. Lean not on our own understanding: Being self-sufficient and trying to figure everything out on our own can lead us astray. We must submit to God, acknowledging that He is in control, and His ways are higher than ours. King Solomon said it best in Proverbs 3:5-6 NIV, "*Trust in the Lord with all your heart and lean not on your own understanding; in all your ways submit to Him, and He will make your paths straight.*"

So, my friend, let's trust God. Let's bravely believe that He will show up when He calls us. Let's unleash our faith, knowing that He will provide, even in the very last moment, because He is the God of breakthrough. If He did it for me, He can do it for you. Embrace these practical ways to activate an eleventh-hour miracle and watch as God works wonders in your life and breaks down all your fears that He might not be sufficient. He is everything you need, in every moment. Don't let your fear tell you otherwise. Stand firm on the truth of His Word.

Chapter 5

Faith Makes Miracles:
Fear of Leaving Your Comfort Zone

Not all of us can do great things, but we can do small things with great love. ~ Mother Teresa of Calcutta

WHEN YOU TAKE THE BOLD STEP of saying yes to God, you will see miracles along the way. These miracles unfold daily if we open our eyes to see them. Unfortunately, we often find ourselves insulated from God's movement and work due to our reliance on our jobs, income, insurance, and retirement plans. We forget to lean on God for all our needs and become too comfortable relying on our paychecks and leaving little room for activating our faith. However, true dedication to saying yes to God demands that we step out of our comfort zone and expect miracles to accompany us on this profound journey.

> ...true dedication to saying yes to God demands that we step out of our comfort zone and expect miracles to accompany us on this profound journey.

Stepping beyond our comfort zone demands effort and courage. It urges us to venture into the unknown, trusting in God's plans and purposes even when the way ahead remains obscured. Yet, it is precisely when we take that step that extraordinary things unfold. We unearth talents and abilities we never knew we possessed, and we experience the overwhelming joy and fulfillment that comes from serving God.

The truth is, many of us become so content in our familiar lives that we resist leaving our comfort zones. The fear of change holds us back from exploring greater possibilities that God may have in store for us. Sometimes, He calls us to embrace paths we never thought possible, urging us to step out of our comfort zones and follow Him with unwavering devotion.

When we leave our comfort zones, we must be prepared to take risks and relinquish our fears and doubts to embrace God's divine plan for our lives. It requires a resolute commitment to saying yes to God, even if it means sacrificing our desires and dreams for His greater purpose.

I vividly recall the day I said YES to God, embarking on a journey beyond my comfort zone. My fears didn't vanish automatically; I had to activate my faith. I had to fulfill what God called me to do, even in moments of trepidation. Through this experience, I learned that faith is the antidote to fear, and having faith is imperative to stepping beyond our comfort zones and witnessing miracles.

Miracles have unfolded before our very eyes, and Jesus has come through for us time and time again, often just when we needed it most.

One such remarkable moment occurred when we embarked on establishing Open Arms. Initially, we only had funds to care for five children in the house we purchased. Though it was a small beginning, we believed that those five children in our care were far better off than they would have been on the streets or in an orphanage.

As we found sponsors to support these five children, we gradually expanded and took in more children. Our ministry grew to care for around twenty five children, and we believed that we were making a significant impact. However, as our ministry expanded further, we needed to witness even more miracles. We sought more churches to join us on mission trips and more sponsors to support our cause. We cried out to God, asking for His miraculous provision.

One day, while teaching a devotional to the kids, I shared a story

WHEN WE LEAVE OUR COMFORT ZONES, WE MUST BE PREPARED TO TAKE RISKS AND RELINQUISH OUR FEARS AND DOUBTS TO EMBRACE GOD'S DIVINE PLAN FOR OUR LIVES. IT REQUIRES A RESOLUTE COMMITMENT TO SAYING YES TO GOD, EVEN IF IT MEANS SACRIFICING OUR DESIRES AND DREAMS FOR HIS GREATER PURPOSE.

about a missionary in Africa named Heidi Baker, who had seen God provide miraculously through Iris Ministries for hundreds of children in Africa. The kids remarked that she was my "tocaya," my name twin, and they eagerly expressed their faith in God's ability to do great things for us, just as He had done for her. Inspired by their faith, we decided to take an offering for Heidi Baker's ministry, even though our resources were limited at that point.

I asked the children if they wanted to contribute, and one brave little girl, about eight years old, excitedly ran to her backpack and gave me twenty pesos, which was equivalent to about one dollar. Other children followed suit, donating their lunch money and whatever coins they had in their pockets. Collectively, we gathered a little over ten dollars, along with the one hundred dollars I had set aside to give at Heidi Baker's conference. We fervently prayed over this offering, laying our hands on it and crying out to God to multiply it miraculously, not just for our needs but also for the needs of the children in Africa and Mexico.

As we concluded our prayer with a resounding "Amen," our cook, Mari, burst into the room, filled with joyous excitement. She urged me to come quickly to the kitchen, and as we rushed there, we saw the rice and beans overflowing from their pots. Mari was astounded, as she had only prepared half the usual amount, yet the food overflowed. We couldn't contain our delight, jumping and embracing each other in a circle of gratitude for the miracle we had just witnessed. I eagerly fetched the children, who had fervently prayed for miracles moments before, to show them that God answers prayers and is still in the business of performing miracles.

Experiencing such a powerful moment of divine provision reinforced our faith and affirmed that God is the same yesterday, today, and forever (Hebrews 13:8). His miracles are not limited by time or place but are available to all His children, wherever they may be. As we continued our journey of saying yes to God, we learned that with faith and obedience, even the most daunting of challenges can be transformed into remarkable opportunities for God's miracles to shine through. Faith makes miracles.

| Faith makes miracles.

Above and Beyond Anything you Could Imagine

Our faith grew that day, and our fear of not having enough was losing its grip. We continued to work, and we continued to grow. By the grace of God, we purchased three more lots on the side of our existing building, and in 2009, during the collapse of the US economy, we built a 6,000 sq. ft. building. We declared, "We are not in crisis; we are in Christ!" Miraculously, people gave and came to build. We saw miracle after miracle right in front of our eyes. Only God could do something like this. Only God can make a way, in the downfall of the economy, and build another building to take in more children and help more families.

Once we opened this new building, we accepted more and more children. With more kids, we saw more need. But we also saw more miracles. Jesus always showed up on time and has miraculously provided above and beyond anything we could ever dream or imagine (Ephesians 3:20-21).

"We are not in crisis; we are in Christ!"

In 2011, we expected a mission team to come and help us continue building and ministering to the children. When mission teams come, we make delicious home cooked Mexican meals, including home-made flour tortillas. The group was large. Maybe seventy five people, and my two cooks couldn't manage all the cooking. We hired a lady in the community to make us 400 flour tortillas. I was busy with the logistics when Mari, our cook, came to me crying and said, "The tortilla lady is sick, and she couldn't make the tortillas. I don't know what we are going to do. The group is supposed to eat in one hour, and we aren't going to have any tortillas." This is a significant problem in Mexico; not having tortillas was almost a sin. I grabbed her hands and prayed that God would show up yet again. I said God will provide like He always does. She looked at me, agreed, and returned to making the yummiest Mexican food you could ever eat. I thought, "Okay, God, I don't know how you will do this, but we need 400 flour tortillas. I know I can go to the store and buy corn tortillas, but God, you know it is not the same." I was too busy trying to get work and ministry projects running with the mission team and delegating jobs to our staff, so I couldn't dwell on our lack. At that moment, I had no option but to believe God would show up.

About twenty minutes later, a lady from our local church visited and brought her daughter and son-in-law from Tijuana to take a quick tour of the ministry. It was a pleasant surprise to see them, and we welcomed them on campus. Before I could give them a tour, she said, "Heidi, my daughter and her husband who are here with me own a flour tortilla factory and brought you 400 flour tortillas. We hope you can use them." I stopped in my tracks, wide eyes and mouth agape. I said, "You are kidding right?" She said, "No, why would I be kidding." I began to weep and took them into the kitchen to tell my cook. We stood there crying as yet again, God provided miraculously, right on time.

Leaving our comfort zone isn't merely about embracing change or taking risks; it opens the floodgates to witness a profound move of God. Stepping beyond the familiar terrain of our lives positions us to experience His power and presence in extraordinary ways. When we shed the security of the known and venture into the unknown, we create room for God to work wonders in our lives and in the lives of others. It is in these moments of vulnerability and faith-filled obedience that God's transformative grace shines brightest.

His miracles abound when we say yes to Him, releasing us from the confines of self-reliance and ushering us into the realm of divine intervention. Leaving our comfort zone isn't just an act of bravery; it is an invitation for God to reveal Himself in ways we could never have fathomed, moving our hearts, transforming circumstances, and igniting a flame of hope and inspiration for all who witness His mighty works.

> Leaving our comfort zone isn't merely about embracing change or taking risks; it opens the floodgates to witness a profound move of God.

Fear to Faith

Our ministry multiplied as God provided miraculously. With the care of seventy five children, we extended our reach even further, establishing a medical and dental facility to accommodate visiting doctors and dentists. We took a leap of faith and planted a church on our campus, appointing dedicated pastors to lead our growing congregation. The formation of a thriving youth ministry became a beacon of hope for the lost teens of La Misión. Every step of the way, we relied on the unwavering belief in God's daily provision, through the Body of Christ. Our dependence on Him was absolute. Without His intervention, we could not provide food for the children, gas for the school bus, electricity, or running water. Each day required God to show up, and He never disappointed. As the ministries thrived and a sense of comfort began to set in, God's voice beckoned us towards another quest, into another community. He whispered to me, "Heidi, I have never called you to be comfortable. Get ready to open your arms to more children and families in another community." He urged us to extend our arms further, to love more children, embrace more families, and embark on a fresh journey of keeping families together. It was a call to leave the familiar once more, and to relinquish comfort for a greater purpose.

I distinctly remember the moment those words reached my heart. My husband had returned from a mission trip to the San Quintin Valley, and as I sat on my bed praying for him and the mission team, God was preparing me for the next steps in our family and ministry. In that sacred moment of prayer, God's voice resonated clearly, urging me to "get ready." I instinctively knew what He meant—an expansion was on the horizon. While my heart had already embraced the idea, fear tried to hold me back. The thought of starting anew, raising more funds, and managing the logistics frightened me. But God reminded me that I was brave, called, and destined for this very purpose.

> I have never called you to be comfortable.

When Daniel returned from that mission trip, he recounted the desperate need in the community they visited, including children wandering the streets, some without shoes. He saw the potential for a second campus there, and despite my apprehensions, his words echoed what God had already been whispering to me. Fear tried to grip me, thinking of the financial implications and the changes it would entail, but God's reminder refocused my perspective. Fear makes us look inward, taking our eyes off Jesus, but God reassured me, just as He reassures all of us in times of fear: "*Take courage! It is I. Don't be afraid*" (Mathew 14:27 NIV).

I found solace in the story of Peter walking on water in Matthew 14:22-33. Just like Peter, we may waver in fear when we take our eyes off Jesus and focus on the obstacles before us. Jesus reaches out to catch us, lovingly reprimanding us for our limited faith and our doubts. He has caught me countless times when fear clouded my faith in His plans for my life. His reassuring hand reminds me that if He has called me, He will be with me every step of the way.

I believe He is saying this to you too—wherever you are called, He will be there with you, catching you when your faith falters and guiding you from fear to faith. So, embrace your calling, step out of the boat, and discover the depths of His unfailing love and grace. He will catch you, just like he did for Peter, and just like he did for me. You, my dear friend, can step out of the boat and go from fear to faith.

> ...wherever you are called, He will be there with you, catching you when your faith falters and guiding you from fear to faith.

Faith Takes Action

Soon after my husband returned from that impactful mission trip, he knew it was crucial for me to witness the need in the San Quintin Valley myself. He understood that seeing the situation first-hand would quell my lingering fears, igniting a deeper sense of faith within me. As we journeyed along the bumpy, dirt roads, my heart sank at the sight before me—children wandering the streets, families in desperate need of support, and orphanages brimming with children whose parents longed for assistance. The need was undeniable, and my heart broke once more for these innocent children in crisis. Exploring various communities, we began to envision the possibilities of opening a second campus, extending a helping hand to even more children and families. My heart overflowed with hope and determination, and upon our return, we fervently sought God's guidance.

Shortly after this trip, Daniel started taking the youth group from La Misión to build a home for a family in need, and our connection to the San Quintin Valley deepened. We gradually recognized that the Open Arms model had the potential to be replicated in any pueblo, transcending not only Mexico but the entirety of Latin

America. It became clear to me that Open Arms had the capacity to address numerous challenges and meet a multitude of needs.

We returned to the San Quintin Valley several times, our hearts brimming with a sense of purpose and divine direction. On one of those journeys back to La Misión, we found ourselves lost in contemplation, attempting to process the enormity of what lay ahead and discern God's leading. Breaking the silence, Daniel looked at me and asked, "Where do you feel God is leading us?" To my surprise, I felt a stirring within, and without hesitation, I replied, "I don't know why, but I feel something for Camalú." Astonishingly, Daniel's eyes lit up, and he responded, "Really? Me too." In that profound moment, we realized that God was unequivocally speaking to us both, confirming the path we were to take.

> ...hearts were anchored in the knowledge that if God called us to it, He would provide every step of the way.

Trusting in God's divine plan, we set our hearts on Camalú ready to embrace the new community with open arms and boundless love. As the vision of a second campus in Camalú began to materialize, we braced ourselves for the challenges that lay ahead. Yet, our hearts were anchored in the knowledge that if God called us to it, He would provide every step of the way. The journey of saying yes to God once more was a testament to His faithfulness and a profound reminder that when we dare to leave our comfort zones, extraordinary opportunities for His miraculous work unfold before us. And so, with unwavering faith and hearts open to new horizons, we embraced the next chapter in our lives and ministry, fully trusting that God's presence would continue to guide and sustain us on this remarkable path of obedience and transformation.

In Camalú, the harsh reality is that eighty percent of the people are migrant workers from Oaxaca and other southern states, toiling in the agricultural fields and earning a meager fifteen dollars a day, on average. Amidst these circumstances, their children become the biggest victims. Older siblings, forfeit their education to stay at home to take care of their younger siblings while their parents labor in the fields. The consequences of such hardships are grave—hunger and the lack of childcare stand as the top complaints among mothers.

The absence of adequate childcare programs in Mexico leaves countless children vulnerable, unsupervised, and left to roam the streets without anyone to care for them. This distressing reality demanded action, compelling us to confront the injustice and suffering before a child is hurt, abused, and abandoned. Micah 6:8 echoes in our hearts, urging us to *"act justly, love mercy, and walk humbly with God."* The children in Camalú, abandoned on the streets or left in orphanages, represent some of the most vulnerable children in the world. It is an unimaginable thought—leaving your kids home alone, exposed to countless dangers such as child trafficking, sexual abuse by neighbors, or even accidental fires as witnessed in the tragedy of that couple in Tijuana. The psychological impact of being abandoned at an orphanage is yet another burden they might bear. The weight of these circumstances was undeniable, and our hearts were resolute, ready to take this daring leap of faith.

With a firm belief that God had led us to Camalú, we knew we had to take action to break the cycle of suffering and neglect. We needed to provide a haven of love, care, and opportunity for these vulnerable children. Our hearts aligned with the urgent call to transform their lives, to ensure that they are nurtured, educated, and protected from the harsh realities they had endured thus far. The journey ahead was laden with challenges and uncertainties, but we were fortified by the conviction that every child deserves a chance to flourish, to be embraced by the warmth of a loving family, and to discover their God-given potential.

As we set out on this new mission, we were reminded that

stepping beyond our comfort zone wasn't merely about fulfilling our own desires. It was about embracing God's heart for the marginalized and responding to His call to love our neighbors as ourselves.

It was time to unleash our bravery yet again, and take yet another leap of faith, knowing that every child we touched, every life we impacted, would be a testament to the miraculous power of saying yes to God's call, even when it required stepping into the unknown and facing the most daunting challenges. Together, we embarked on this new chapter of love, hope, and transformation. We were trusting that God's unwavering presence would illuminate our path and empower us to make a lasting difference in the lives of the precious children and families in Camalú.

Facing Opposition with Deep Conviction

During one of our visits to Camalú, we felt compelled to seek insight from the director of a local orphanage in Vicente Guerrero, located just twenty five minutes south of Camalú. We eagerly shared our vision with him and inquired about the situation in Camalú. His response was disheartening—he cautioned us against going to Camalú, describing it as "hard ground" where no ministry had ever survived. He pointed out that the churches in the area were small, and the population was composed of individuals from diverse backgrounds, each holding distinct beliefs and ideologies. Despite his discouraging words, we couldn't shake the conviction in our hearts. We walked out of that meeting, looked at each other, and said, "Well, it looks like Camalú needs Jesus. Let's go."

In that moment, we couldn't help but draw parallels to the biblical account of the twelve spies sent by Moses to explore the land of Canaan. Just as ten spies returned with reports of giants and insurmountable challenges, there were voices warning us about the difficulties in Camalú. However, like Joshua and Caleb, who

IT WAS TIME TO UNLEASH OUR BRAVERY YET AGAIN, AND TAKE YET ANOTHER LEAP OF FAITH, KNOWING THAT EVERY CHILD WE TOUCHED, EVERY LIFE WE IMPACTED, WOULD BE A TESTAMENT TO THE MIRACULOUS POWER OF SAYING YES TO GOD'S CALL, EVEN WHEN IT REQUIRED STEPPING INTO THE UNKNOWN AND FACING THE MOST DAUNTING CHALLENGES.

remained steadfast in their faith and trusted in God's promises, we chose to be resolute. Despite the negative report, we knew deep within that God was calling us to Camalú. My husband, Daniel, boldly declared and prophesied that Camalú was a land flowing with milk and honey, rebuking the claim of it being hard ground. Together, we decided to embrace a perspective of unwavering belief in God's power to do great and mighty things in Camalú, in its people, and through the work of Open Arms.

> Our determination to stand as Joshua and Caleb, refusing to be swayed by fear or negativity, became a testament to our unyielding trust in God's divine plan.

As we set out on this daunting journey, we recognized that challenges and opposition might come our way. Yet, our faith in God's guiding hand and the knowledge that we were fulfilling His purpose spurred us forward. We knew that with God on our side, we could overcome any obstacle and witness His miraculous work in the lives of these vulnerable children and their families. Our determination to stand as Joshua and Caleb, refusing to be swayed by fear or negativity, became a testament to our unyielding trust in God's divine plan.

Camalú needed Jesus, and we were ready to be His instruments of love, hope, and transformation in this seemingly difficult terrain. Armed with faith and the power of God's unfailing love, we embraced the challenge before us, squashed the fear that tried to rise within us, and aligned ourselves with God's will for our lives and ministry. Our hearts were filled with hope, knowing that we were answering the call to shine a light in the darkest corners and to bring the message of God's redeeming grace to those needing it the most.

True Love Casts Out All Fear

The journey of believing again and starting anew was intimidating for me. Moments of tears, anxiety, and tension enveloped my soul as I wrestled with the terrifying task of raising enough funds to purchase land and construct a sizable building, all while keeping our first campus running smoothly. In the midst of my uncertainties, my loving Father God tenderly spoke to my spirit, gently reassuring me, "Heidi, I have never called you to be comfortable. Get ready and believe in me for the miraculous again."

My deep love for Jesus and knowing Him as my Father, made it easier to put my trust in Him. I was willing to follow Him anywhere, regardless of the cost. 1 John 3:1a NIV says, "See what great love the Father has lavished on us, that we should be called children of God! And that is what we are!" Embracing this truth should inspire us to live as Jesus lived—a life marked by radical love. For He loves me so immensely, why wouldn't I trust Him over and over again? As I dreamt alongside the Dream Giver, I understood that His dreams were beyond what I could accomplish alone. Mark Batterson's words in his book "Chase *the Lion*" echoed in my heart: "If your dream doesn't scare you, it's too small."[1] Well, this dream of building a second campus in Camalú genuinely terrified me. In a moment of prayer, I poured out my fears to God, likening the situation to having only one dollar in my pocket all over again. I asked for another sign, seeking reassurance of God's provision. "God, I will go, even if I am scared," I prayed, "Just show me that you will provide for all the needs at our first campus and enough to build our second." In response, God directed me to check the PayPal account. It was an unusual step for me, as I typically left such matters to our bookkeeper. Nevertheless, I followed His prompt, and to

> "God, I will go, even if I am scared,"...

my astonishment, there it was—a generous donation of $20,000 on the very day I cried out to God for miraculous provision. This act of obedience from a person who had no knowledge of our prayers or our plans for a second campus confirmed God's faithfulness once more. My faith soared and my fear dissolved as my love for the Lord deepened.

We can depend on the truth of I John 4:18a NIV, *"There is no fear in love. But perfect love drives out fear."* God's boundless love and unwavering faithfulness nullify any reason for fear. The day I said *yes* to God again, the day I chose to believe in His provision became a turning point. He has shown up at every step of the way since then. Faith assures me that God is already ahead of me, regardless of the future.

> God's boundless love and unwavering faithfulness nullify any reason for fear.

From that day on, I have never stopped believing that God would provide for Open Arms and me. When we found the land for the Camalú campus, the price of $70,000 for five acres seemed insurmountable. We needed $100,000 to secure the property and begin construction, not to mention the substantial amount required for the 16,000 sq. ft. building. For a boy who grew up in an orphanage and a missionary girl with humble beginnings, raising such a sum appeared astronomical. But my faith was anchored in the God who had multiplied a mere one dollar, and with this unyielding trust, we set forth on a journey marked by God's miraculous provision and love.

100k in 100 days

The call to raise $100K in one hundred days for the Camalu Project became a bold endeavor. We shared God's calling in our newsletter, on social media, and with our supporting churches to raise funds and awareness. The task was daunting, petrifying, actually. But I knew that God had done it before, and He could do it again. Miraculously, in just forty six days, all the money came pouring in, and the Camalu Project was set in motion. We believed. Then obeyed. Then God showed up.

God didn't give us a dream that matched our budget. God was not checking my bank account. He was reviewing our faith. Did we really believe Him? Would we act in faith? If God could close the mouth of lions for Daniel, part the Red Sea for Moses, make the sun stand still for Joshua, send ravens to feed Elijah, open a prison door for Peter, put a baby in the arms of Sarah, and raise Lazarus from the dead, I must believe that He will provide for you and me, too. Nothing you face today is too hard for Him to handle if you believe.

We chose to say *Yes.* Yes to God's calling, yes to facing our fears, and yes to trusting His provision. I said, "Yes, God, I am scared, but we will go scared." "Yes, God send me." "Yes, God, but you better show up." Glory

> God didn't give us a dream that matched our budget. God was not checking my bank account.

to God He did. We don't have a plan B. We only have a plan A. Our plan is to depend on God and God alone. We rarely have fundraisers. We don't have a marketing team. We have God, and we have His people who have also believed.

He has taken two ordinary people and has done the extraordinary because we believed Him. There is power in your belief in God. Don't underestimate what God can do when you believe in Him and believe in His Promises. We had no backup plan, no alternatives; our sole reliance was on God and His people.

The Camalú Project exceeded our wildest dreams. It became a refuge for countless children, offering parents a better option than leaving their kids home alone or sending them to orphanages due to poverty. God ordained the family, and we stood firm, fighting for these families, believing that God would use us to provide for the least of these, just as Jesus opened His arms to us.

On November 1st, 2016, we opened the doors to the first twenty five children, and the number quickly grew to one hundred. Among them were two remarkable boys, Raul and Miguel Angel. Their story is all too common: a single mother and a migrant worker with nowhere to take her children while she toiled in the agricultural fields. Their mom had no family in Camalú and nowhere to take her children. She would lock them in their little shack, where Raul would care for his baby brother. Their mom would leave for work around 5:00 a.m., so the kids would still be asleep. When the sun came up, Raul would wake up, get ready, change his brother's diaper, get him dressed, cook him an egg on their two-burner camping stove, and take care of him throughout the day. Raul was only six years old. He wasn't going to school. He was Miguel's caretaker. Additionally, to make ends meet, their mom would take her boys out to the streets and sell trinkets to the passersby to make extra income. Before we opened the childcare center, their mom begged us for help. She was worried about what could happen to her boys during the day, and worried that the child protective services would come and take them to an orphanage.

Upon learning of their plight, we knew we had to take this family in immediately. Now, under our care, Raul and Miguel were safe from the threat of being sent to an orphanage, and, more importantly, they were introduced to the love of Jesus for the first time. Sadly, their story is just one among many, but it serves as a poignant reminder of the transformation that occurs when we step out in faith and embrace the call to love and care for those in need. By saying yes to Jesus and leaving our comfort zone, lives like Raul and Miguel's will forever be changed.

Lives Are Changed When You Live
Outside of Your Comfort Zone

Not only does your life change when you say yes to Jesus, but many lives are also changed because of your yes. I want to encourage you. Do you see the word "courage" there? Encourage means to "inspire with courage, spirit, or hope."[2] Friends, my hope through my story is that I can encourage you to unleash your bravery. You too can take courage. You too can conquer the fear of stepping out of your comfort zone. Stand on God's promises for your life. Remember Deuteronomy 31:6 NIV, *"Be strong and courageous. Do not be afraid or terrified because of them, for the LORD your God goes with you; he will never leave you or forsake you."*

My faith has been built up and has grown these last twenty years on the mission field, but my faith-building days are not over. I encounter worry at times, but I wouldn't want to be anywhere else but in complete dependence on God.

We are called to depend on Him today and only on Him for everything. Many times, we have insulated ourselves from miracles, from seeing God manifest Himself in absolutely tangible ways because we put our dependence on our jobs, our spouse, our paycheck, and our insurance rather than our Creator. Every good thing comes from Him, so why don't we depend on Him for everything?

> I encounter worry at times, but I wouldn't want to be anywhere else but in complete dependence on God.

I am the most disqualified person to be doing what I am doing. I was filled with fear. I was living in sin before moving to the mission field. I had no resources and married an orphan. Most of us feel unworthy or disqualified from being used by God. Saying yes to Jesus can be challenging. There are times when it requires sacrifice,

SAYING YES TO JESUS CAN BE CHALLENGING. THERE ARE TIMES WHEN IT REQUIRES SACRIFICE, PERSEVERANCE, AND COURAGE. THERE ARE TIMES WHEN YOU HAVE TO FACE YOUR FEARS, YOUR DOUBTS, AND YOUR WEAKNESSES. BUT THERE IS NO GREATER JOY THAN FOLLOWING JESUS AND NO GREATER PEACE THAN TRUSTING IN HIS PLANS FOR OUR LIVES. GOD WILL EMBOLDEN YOU TO FULFILL THE CALL ON YOUR LIFE.

perseverance, and courage. There are times when you have to face your fears, your doubts, and your weaknesses. But there is no greater joy than following Jesus and no greater peace than trusting in His plans for our lives. God will embolden you to fulfill the call on your life.

If you feel the call to say yes to Jesus and to step out of your comfort zone, I encourage you to take that step of faith. Don't let fear hold you back. Don't let doubt or insecurity rob you of the blessings that come with surrendering to His will. Say yes to Jesus and see what amazing things He has in store for you.

Living outside your comfort zone can be scary and intimidating, but it is also where the most growth and change can happen. Venturing beyond what is familiar allows us to explore uncharted territories and embrace opportunities we wouldn't have stumbled upon otherwise. This statement holds especially true in terms of our spiritual journey. As believers, we are summoned to walk in Jesus' footsteps and spread His love. However, this often requires us to step beyond our usual boundaries and do things that may not come naturally or feel comfortable. Maybe it means sharing the gospel with a stranger, volunteering in a new ministry, or forgiving someone who has hurt you deeply. Whatever it may be, it requires you to leave the safety and security of your comfort zone and trust that God will be with you every step of the way.

The truth is, when we live outside of our comfort zone, lives are changed—both our own and the lives of those around us. By taking risks and stepping out in faith, we allow God to work in and through us in ways we could never imagine. We become vessels of His grace and love and can impact the world for His kingdom.

Think about the early disciples of Jesus. They left their homes, families, and comfort zones to follow Him. They faced persecution, rejection, and even death for the gospel's sake. But their willingness to live outside of their comfort zones changed the course of history.

The message of salvation spread worldwide, and countless lives were transformed.

Of course, living outside of our comfort zone takes work. It requires us to be brave, vulnerable, and willing to embrace uncertainty. But the rewards are immeasurable. We discover our true strength and resilience. We deepen our relationship with God and encounter the joy and fruitfulness that comes from living a life of purpose.

If you feel glued to your comfort zone, know there is so much more waiting for you when you step out. Trust that God is with you every step of the way and take that first step into the unknown. Through our willingness to explore uncharted territories with the Lord, we can witness the extraordinary power of God's love changing lives, one courageous step at a time.

Faith makes miracles but fear buries callings. Trust that God is with you every step of the way, and take that first step into the unknown. It's time. Unleash your bravery because your life, and the lives of those around you, will be forever changed.

> **Faith makes miracles but fear buries callings.**

Chapter 6
NO! I Can't Let Go:
The Paralyzing Fear of Losing Control

You can have faith or you can have control, but you cannot have both. If you want God to do something off the chart, you have to take your hands off the controls. ~ Mark Batterson.

HAVE YOU EVER FELT like your life was spinning out of control, like you were caught in a whirlwind and couldn't find your footing? This feeling of helplessness is a common experience for many people, and it can be incredibly scary.

The fear of losing control can be paralyzing. It can leave you feeling vulnerable, exposed, and powerless. As a result, you may find yourself constantly worrying about things that are out of your control which can significantly impact your mental and emotional well-being.

One of the reasons why losing control can be so terrifying is that it forces us to confront our limitations. We like to think of ourselves as capable and in charge, but the truth is that we are all vulnerable to the unexpected. No matter how much we plan or prepare, there will always be things we cannot predict or control.

Another reason losing control can be scary is that it can lead to negative consequences. When we feel like we're not in charge, we may make impulsive decisions or take risks that we wouldn't normally take. This can lead to mistakes or even dangerous situations, eroding our sense of control and safety.

The truth is, though, the fear of

> ...the fear of losing control is often worse than the actual experience.

losing control is often worse than the actual experience. When faced with an unexpected challenge or setback, we often find ourselves more resilient and capable than we thought. We may need to adjust our expectations or approach, but we can usually find a way forward.

Tight Grasp to Control

In the Bible, there are many stories of people who faced the fear of losing control. One example is the story of Moses. If there is anyone in the Bible I relate to the most, it is Moses, who God called to lead the Israelites out of slavery in Egypt. Moses was reluctant to take on this task, but obeyed God. However, even though he was doing what God had called him to do, he faced many challenges that were out of his control. After Moses said yes to God's plan and will to be the deliverer of the Israelites from the hands of the Egyptians, he led them into the desert, where the Israelites grumbled and complained. They rebelled against Moses, and they even wanted to stone him. Moses cried to God, *"And Moses said to the Lord, 'Why are you treating me, your servant, so harshly? Have mercy on me! What did I do to deserve the burden of all these people?'"* (Numbers 11:11, NLT). Moses seemed overwhelmed and powerless. He cried out to God for help when things got out of his control.

In the pages of the Bible, we find a resounding truth: God is in control of everything. His sovereignty reigns over all aspects of life, and nothing occurs outside of His watchful eye. Even when we feel like we are losing control, we can find comfort and reassurance in the knowledge that God remains firmly in control. His plans for our lives are perfect, even when we don't fully comprehend the unfolding events.

Nevertheless, many of us, myself included, struggle with letting go of control and allowing God to take the lead at times. Have you ever clung tightly to something or someone only to realize that your grasp caused more harm than good? I certainly have. The seeds of this struggle were planted during my parents' divorce, when everything seemed to spiral out of control. It was then that I adopted the belief that I needed to take matters into my own hands to protect myself from further pain. The illusion of control gave me a false sense of security, allowing me to keep others at arm's length to shield myself from potential hurt. As a Christian, I understand the importance of surrendering my control to Jesus, acknowledging that His ways are superior to my own. My journey on the mission field has pushed me far beyond my comfort zone, leaving me feeling vulnerable and afraid. It's an admission I don't shy away from. When confronted with the possibility of losing control, my instinct is to cling tightly to whatever semblance of control I can find.

Amidst this struggle, I have also come to realize that true freedom lies in letting go and trusting God's unfailing guidance. I've experienced the immense power of faith in God's plan, even when it requires me to surrender control. Through my journey, I've learned that by loosening my grip, I open myself to God's wisdom and providence. It's not an easy process, but as I continually lean on Him, I find my fears subsiding, replaced by a deep sense of peace that can only come from trusting the Creator of the universe.

Tight Reins

As we settled into our second campus in Camalú, I found myself grappling with a sense of being utterly out of control—the most intense feeling since the day I first moved to Mexico. Relocating our family from La Misión to Camalú was a necessary step, given the increased demands of our new campus. While I rejoiced in the miraculous provision for this new campus, where countless children could find safety and refuge, I also mourned leaving behind the staff who had become like family and the children I had grown so fond of over the years. I knew we would continue to commute between the two campuses, even though it was a three-hour drive, but it meant saying goodbye to a familiar life that had shaped me for over a decade.

The fear of the unknown enveloped my mind like a swarm of bees, buzzing with uncertainty. A swarm of bees is usually not aggressive unless provoked. When I feel out of control, watch out because this momma bee might sting you. I have a t-shirt that says, "Not fragile like a flower, fragile like a bomb." Sometimes an explosion is just waiting to happen. This is a flaw and sin that I am not proud of because, in the end, grasping for control myself rather than surrendering it to God can lead to hurt and pain for others.

The burden of wanting to be involved in every aspect of both campuses weighed heavily on me. Some days, I found myself feeling like I could take on the role of Octomom, handling multiple tasks at once, and, at times, I even believed I could be a superwoman, capable of doing it all. But reality set in, and I had to acknowledge that I am just one person striving to follow God wholeheartedly, and my human limitations often hinder me more than I care to admit. My fear of losing control was becoming overwhelming, clouding my thoughts and actions.

Deep down, I knew I had to empower my staff to make more decisions on their own, but it felt like loosening the reins that I had been clutching so tightly. Internally, I struggled with letting go of my first ministry location, the baby that God had entrusted to us. It was where I started my life as a married woman and where we raised our precious daughters. Letting go was not an easy task. I had to remind myself that everything is on loan from God, and nothing truly belongs to me. However, relying on others while being absent as the leader was challenging. I had to come to terms with this reality, or I would push my staff to leave, and I would be left with more anxiety.

I recall a defining moment when my lead staff person decided on a paint color for the kitchen, as a mission team was scheduled to repaint it. Without consulting me, she chose a paint color, but when I saw it, I couldn't help but express my disapproval. I promptly went online, searching for what I deemed to be a "better" and "more suitable" color at Home Depot. In doing so, I inadvertently belittled her judgment, and the aftermath left her hesitant to make any more decisions on her own. I recognized the importance of her developing decision-making skills, yet relinquishing control, even over minor choices like paint colors, proved challenging. Despite acknowledging the need to let go, my distance of three hours heightened my sense of powerlessness, prompting me to grasp onto any semblance of control available.

Spiraling Out of Control

Life felt like I was being trapped on a roller coaster, hurtling through unpredictable twists and turns, with my grip on control slipping away. As much as I clung to the safety bar, I realized that my attempts to navigate life on my own were futile without divine intervention. It was a moment of surrender, a humbling recognition that only by trusting in God's plan could I find peace amidst the chaos. Proverbs 3:5-6 NIV became my guiding light: "*Trust in the Lord with all your heart and lean not on your own understanding; in all your ways submit to him, and he will make your paths straight.*" When we let go and place our trust in God, even in the face of uncertainty, He leads us on the right path.

In my struggle to relinquish control, I acknowledged my faults and the pain I caused others. Crying out to God for help, I sought healing from my control issues. I didn't want to make all the decisions or undermine the trust of my staff. I longed to lead with humility and faith in God's guidance. Healing and growth were necessary, and I understood that as leaders, we can only give what we possess. Seeking God's healing and restoration, I learned that we must not dwell in the past but keep advancing as God calls us. The promise in Hebrews 13:5-6 NIV reassured me, *"Never will I leave you; never will I forsake you."* With this confidence, I proclaimed, *"The Lord is my helper; I will not be afraid. What can mere mortals do to me?"* (Hebrews 13:6). God's faithful presence would accompany me every step of the way, as Psalms 27:1 NIV affirmed, *"The Lord is my light and my salvation—whom shall I fear? The Lord is the stronghold of my life—of whom shall I be afraid?"*

If you find yourself grappling with the fear of losing control in any aspect of life—whether it's relationships, career, ministry, or the future—I hope my journey serves as a cautionary tale. I made mistakes, struggled to trust, and faltered in my decisions. Yet, through countless failures and attempts, I finally stepped off the chaotic roller coaster, entrusted my team with leadership, and embraced the truth that God's ways are higher and wiser than my own. Letting go and letting God became more than a cliche—it became a transformative principle that set me free from the chains of fear and allowed His purpose to unfold in remarkable ways. Remember, God's guidance is unwavering, and His love casts out all fear. Embrace His plan, trust in His wisdom, and watch as He takes you on a journey beyond your wildest expectations.

> Letting go and letting God became more than a cliche—it became a transformative principle that set me free from the chains of fear and allowed His purpose to unfold in remarkable ways.

The Dangers of Control

As I was struggling with control, God led me to read the story of David and Bathsheba in 2 Samuel 11. I immediately realized I didn't want to make horrendous mistakes like King David. King David was a man after God's own heart, but he was also a man who struggled with sin, temptation, and control. One of his most significant lapses in judgment came when he saw Bathsheba, the wife of Uriah the Hittite, bathing on a rooftop. Despite knowing she was married, David gave in to his desire and slept with her, leading to her pregnancy.

When David realized that Bathsheba was carrying his child, he panicked. He knew that if the news got out, he would face severe consequences, including punishment under the law of Moses. So, he hatched a plan to cover up his sin by bringing Uriah home from the battlefield and encouraging him to sleep with his wife, hoping that people would believe the child was Uriah's.

King David's control issues were at the root of his bad decisions. They stemmed from his desire to cover up his sin and maintain his reputation. David was a man accustomed to having power and control over others. As a king, he had the authority to make decisions that impacted the lives of countless people. But when he committed adultery with Bathsheba, he realized that his actions could have serious consequences for himself and his kingdom.

Instead of confronting his sin and seeking forgiveness, David resorted to manipulation and control. When Uriah refused to sleep with his wife, remaining faithful to his fellow soldiers in battle, David's attempts to control the situation intensified. In a desperate move, he devised a more extreme plan, sending Uriah back to the battlefield with instructions for his comrades to abandon him.

David's relentless need for control blinded him to the gravity of his actions, consumed by the desire to conceal his sin at any cost.

In his quest to cover up the affair, he tragically orchestrated Uriah's death, not only committing murder but also betraying the loyalty of a devoted soldier.

David's story serves as a cautionary reminder of the dangers of control, demonstrating how it can lead us down a path of destruction. When we grasp for control over others, we risk causing harm and inflicting pain on those we should be protecting. My own experiences echo this truth. My hope is that you can learn from both David's and my mistakes. My prayer is that instead of succumbing to the allure of control, let us humbly surrender to God, trusting in His infinite wisdom and boundless grace to lead us on the right path.

> When we grasp for control over others, we risk causing harm and inflicting pain on those we should be protecting.

Letting Go of Control

Letting go of control is undoubtedly a challenging task, but the Bible offers valuable guidance to help us surrender our fears and anxieties to God. Here are some biblical steps to assist you in conquering your fears of letting go of control.

1. Acknowledge that God is ultimately in control of our lives. Proverbs 19:21 emphasizes that despite our plans and desires, it is the Lord's purpose that will prevail.

2. Find peace and reassurance that comes through surrendering our fears and anxieties to God, as urged in Philippians 4:6-7 NIV. *"By presenting our requests to Him in prayer and thanksgiving, we can experience the peace of God that transcends all understanding."*

3. Trust in God's plan. Jeremiah 29:11 assures us that He has a specific plan for each of our lives—a plan to *"prosper [us] and*

give us hope and a future."

4. Align our desires with God's will. Proverbs 3:5-6 urges us to trust in the Lord wholeheartedly and submit to His guidance. By seeking His will, we can find assurance in knowing that He will direct our paths.

5. Release ourselves from the shackles of perfectionism. Ecclesiastes 7:20 reminds us that no one on earth is without sin, emphasizing the reality of human imperfection. By accepting our humanity and embracing the inevitability of mistakes, we can find freedom from the burden of perfectionism.

In embracing these biblical principles, we can embark on a journey of surrender, learning to trust in God's sovereignty and finding peace amidst life's uncertainties. Letting go of control doesn't mean being passive; it means embracing God's divine wisdom and guidance as we navigate the twists and turns of life's journey.

It is a transformative journey, requiring us to surrender our fears and anxieties to God while trusting in His divine plan and seeking His will. It also means freeing ourselves from the burden of perfectionism. Through unwavering faith and fervent prayer, we can find profound peace and reassurance, knowing that God is ultimately in control.

Witnessing the flourishing of our La Misión campus in my absence was a powerful lesson. I had been unwittingly hindering the

> Letting go of control doesn't mean being passive; it means embracing God's divine wisdom and guidance as we navigate the twists and turns of life's journey.

> As the suffocating grip of fear loosened its hold on me, I finally felt the liberating sensation of taking a deep breath and embracing the unknown with renewed courage.

growth of our leaders and staff by my need for control. Once I stepped aside, they flourished, and their leadership skills soared. As the suffocating grip of fear loosened its hold on me, I finally felt the liberating sensation of taking a deep breath and embracing the unknown with renewed courage.

My journey of overcoming the fear of losing control has been both challenging and liberating. I have learned that true strength lies in surrendering to God and trusting in His unfailing love and wisdom. My hope is that my story serves as a reminder that we are not alone in our struggles, and that God's presence and guidance are ever-present, even in the most uncertain times. So, I encourage you to take that leap of faith, to conquer your fears of losing control, and to be brave in embracing God's plan for your life. I am constantly learning to let go of the need to control every outcome, and instead, let God lead me into the abundant life He has prepared for me. Remember the words of Psalm 56:3 NIV, *"When I am afraid, I put my trust in you."* Trust in Him, and you will discover a peace that transcends all understanding. Embrace the adventure of saying yes to Jesus and allow God to work wonders through your surrendered heart. When you release your grip and allow God to take the reins, a realm of endless opportunities and possibilities awaits you.

Chapter 7
My Greatest Fear:
Fear of Being Out God's Will

Do not be afraid. Go and tell my brothers to go to Galilee; there they will see me. ~ Matthew 28:10 NIV

"NO" WITH CAPITAL LETTERS. We were driving in the car when he told me. If I could have jumped out of the moving car and walked away, I would have. "NO. Nope. Not me," I exclaimed sternly!

My brain started racing a million miles a minute. How could my husband even think that pastoring the church at our new campus in Camalú, Baja California, was God's will for our lives? How could he even fathom that I could do all the other things *and* pastor a church. The word pastor is frightening in itself. It is weighty, full of responsibility, not just things to do, but people's souls hang in the balance that pastors are responsible to nurture. It wasn't like I wasn't already in ministry and winning people for the Lord. I was, every day with the children and families we cared for, but pastor? That title wasn't for me. Maybe for my husband, yes. After all, he did graduate from Bible College in 2011, but I did not want to be a pastor (or so I thought).

As I reflect on that tumultuous day, the echoes of our heated argument in the car resonate with regret. The volume of our voices matched the intensity of our clash, and I, in all honesty, failed to display the grace and kindness I wish I had. It's a revelation now that my fear often disguises itself as anger,

> ...my fear often disguises itself as anger, a defense mechanism against the overwhelming uncertainty that creeps in.

a defense mechanism against the overwhelming uncertainty that creeps in. The shockwaves of his unexpected suggestion reverberated through me like a sudden deluge of icy water, leaving me gasping for breath in the suffocating grip of my perceived inadequacy. I was drowning in the overwhelming waves of my own shortcomings, incapable and unqualified to step into the role of a pastor. My plate was already brimming with responsibilities—like overseeing the construction of a new childcare facility—and this unexpected proposition threatened to tip my world off its axis.

Throughout that year, my husband would revisit the topic, hoping for a change of heart. Yet, each time he broached the subject, my immediate response was a vehement rejection. It was as though the very mention of pastoring incited a tumultuous mix of anger, insecurity, and apprehension within me. For a whole year, I adamantly said "NO," both to my husband and, inadvertently, to God. Looking back, I can honestly say that this was the most trying year of my life. I felt a kinship with Moses, struggling to reconcile God's call to lead His people out of Egypt despite his own past transgressions. Could I really be an instrument of God's purpose? Could I effectively preach in Spanish? The burden of juggling my existing commitments while donning this new pastoral mantle was overwhelming. The resounding question lingered: Was God truly calling me?

In the quiet corners of my heart, doubt whispered. I lacked formal training from Bible college, unlike my well-equipped husband. Maybe he could shoulder the responsibility on his own, relegating me to the role of a supportive pastor's wife, content to encourage from the front row without stepping into a high-capacity leadership role. But that was not my personality. I am a go-getter, super slugger, problem-solver, "Put me in coach. I am ready to play!" type of girl. I never wanted to be on the sidelines, especially of what God was doing at Open Arms.

Yet, the fear of inadequacy, the nagging sense of insufficiency, delivered a crippling blow to my core. It was a formidable opponent that immobilized my thoughts and choked my prayers. An overwhelming sense of inadequacy settled in, like an unyielding fog that enshrouded my life. My marriage bore the brunt of the strain. Its fabric fraying under the weight of my internal turmoil. My connection with God grew strained, the intimacy I once cherished now fraught with distance. I was miserable. My marriage was bleeding. My relationship with God was suffering. I felt like I hit a dead end and didn't know what to do. Beneath the visible layer of these apprehensions, a deeper, more potent fear slumbered.

Attitude of Gratitude

When people discuss their greatest fears, the usual suspects often emerge—heights, spiders, snakes—the common phobias that populate our conversations on fear. But if you were to ask me about my most profound fear, it wouldn't involve those typical concerns. No, my greatest fear is being out of the will of God. I am always ready for adrenaline racing activities or brave formidable heights without flinching. Spiders, well, they've met their match in my Mexico journey, and snakes too. However, the prospect of not doing God's will when He has called me, terrifies me to my core. I do not want to go to my right if God is not already there. I do not want to go to the left if God is not already there. I do not want to advance if God is not already there, and going backwards is unthinkable. Discerning His will, for anyone, can sometimes feel daunting, a task that breeds apprehension.

> ...my greatest fear is being out of the will of God.

Avoiding God's will was not my intention, yet I also hesitated to bring my fears before His throne in prayer. I held back from seeking

I DO NOT WANT TO GO TO MY RIGHT IF GOD IS NOT ALREADY THERE. I DO NOT WANT TO GO TO THE LEFT IF GOD IS NOT ALREADY THERE. I DO NOT WANT TO ADVANCE IF GOD IS NOT ALREADY THERE, AND GOING BACKWARDS IS UNTHINKABLE.

His face for an answer, for I dreaded that His will might lead me to the path of pastoring. After many tears and anxious nights, I finally mustered the courage to confront these fears and lay them at the feet of Jesus, or else I knew that true peace would continue to elude me.

The apostle Paul addresses the church in Philippi, offering wisdom on prayer, gratitude, and peace. In Philippians 4:6-7 NIV, his words resonate:

Do not be anxious about anything, but in every situation, by prayer and petition, with thanksgiving, present your requests to God. And the peace of God, which transcends all understanding, will guard your hearts and your minds in Christ Jesus.

Did you catch that? Here, nestled within these words, lies precious insights.

Paul urges us to relinquish anxiety and to bring every situation before God in prayer. Then, he unveils the pivotal truth; *"with thanksgiving."* Then, he discloses the secret—the crucial component that anchors it all. When gratitude intertwines with our petitions, our anxiety takes flight, and in its place settles an indescribable peace. This peace goes

> An attitude of gratitude becomes a conduit for the Prince of Peace to pour out His calming presence.

beyond our comprehension, safeguarding our hearts and minds in the embrace of Christ. Isn't that a staggering revelation? An attitude of gratitude becomes a conduit for the Prince of Peace to pour out His calming presence. This stance of thanksgiving fosters trust in God and kindles a profound peace, even amid the most trying circumstances.

Approaching God with a heart of gratitude redirects our focus from problems to His unwavering goodness and faithfulness. It's a reminder that God has never faltered in the past and will remain steadfast in the future. The outcome? A tranquil oasis within our hearts and minds, even amidst life's tumultuous storms, doubts, or fears.

The time had come for me to pivot my heart toward God, to enter into prayer with a heart overflowing with thankfulness. I was certain that His boundless peace would flow forth abundantly.

The Encounter

It was my birthday, March 10th, 2015. Building had already begun on the property of our second campus. We were living by faith every day and God was showing up; but I was tired of this tug of war with my husband about pastoring. It had been almost a year since our tumultuous argument. I took some time that morning to pray, to be grateful, to ask for God to fill me with His peace, and to be so clear with me whether we *both* were to Pastor the church plant in Camalú. I said, "God, if you really want both Daniel and me to be pastors, I really need a sign." Here I was, acting like Gideon again, and asking for a sign. I love the story of Gideon.

Gideon was a man from the tribe of Manasseh who lived during a time when the Israelites were being oppressed by the Midianites. One day, while threshing wheat in a winepress to hide from the Midianites, an angel of the Lord appeared to Gideon and called him a *"mighty man of valor"* (Judges 6:12, NKJV). Gideon was initially hesitant and doubted that he could lead the Israelites to victory against their oppressors.

To confirm that the angel was truly sent by God, Gideon asked for a sign. He placed a fleece of wool on the ground overnight, and asked God to make the fleece wet with dew while keeping the ground around it dry. When this happened, Gideon still doubted and asked God to reverse the miracle, making the fleece dry and the ground wet, which God also did.

Eventually, Gideon gathered an army of 32,000 men to fight against the Midianites, but God instructed him to reduce the number of soldiers to only 300. Gideon obeyed and led his small but brave army against the Midianites, carrying trumpets and torches concealed in jars.

When they blew their trumpets and broke their jars, the Midianites were thrown into confusion and began fighting each other. Gideon and his army were able to defeat the Midianites and liberate the Israelites from their oppression.

The story of Gideon teaches us that God can use even the most unlikely people to accomplish great things. We may feel weak or inadequate, but if we trust in God and obey His leading, He can use us to make a difference in the world. Like Gideon, we can ask God for signs or confirmation when we are uncertain, and He will be patient and faithful to guide us. Ultimately, the story of Gideon reminds us that with God on our side, we can be brave warriors in the battles of life, no matter how challenging they may be.

Upon concluding my prayer, I cracked open my devotional book by Oswald Chambers, eager to soak in the words of wisdom for the morning. My heart's plea was for God's

> We may feel weak or inadequate, but if we trust in God and obey His leading, He can use us to make a difference in the world.

Word to resound with clarity, revealing His divine path and validating the calling if I was to pastor. Let me share with you, dear friends, that when you put biblical principles into motion, a remarkable shift transpires within the spiritual realm:

Do not be anxious about anything, but in everything, by prayer and petition, with thanksgiving, present your requests to God. ~ Philippians 4:6-7 NIV

As I immersed myself in the devotional's pages, the words

seemed to leap off the paper, spotlighting a verse from Esther 4:14 NIV which ended in the phrase:

You were born for such a time as this.

The Holy Spirit's presence enveloped me, infusing my being with *"a peace that transcends all understanding"* (Philippians 4:7). It was a moment etched with significance—it happened to be my birthday. In the midst of seeking a sign, I found my answer, boldly written in His Word; "Heidi, you were *born* for such a time as this." I heard God say to me at that moment, "I have called you, and if I have called you, I will equip you. It's time to go all-in again." *"Be strong and of a good courage; be not afraid, neither be you dismayed:* for the LORD your God is with you" (Joshua 1:9).

Go and Tell

I wept with gratitude that God was still with me, even though I abandoned Him with my pride, fears, and insecurities. I arose from this encounter with the Holy Spirit, and felt empowered, emboldened, and full of courage, like Mary Magdalene after she encountered the risen Jesus. Let's look at those scriptures:

After the Sabbath, at dawn on the first day of the week, Mary Magdalene and the other Mary went to look at the tomb.

There was a violent earthquake, for an angel of the Lord came down from heaven and, going to the tomb, rolled back the stone and sat on it. His appearance was like lightning, and his clothes were white as snow. The guards were so afraid of him that they shook and became like dead men.

The angel said to the women, "Do not be afraid, for I know that you are looking for Jesus, who was crucified. He is not here; he has risen, just as he said. Come and see the place where he lay. Then go quickly and tell his disciples: 'He has risen from the dead and is going ahead of you into Galilee. There you will see him.' Now I have told you."

So the women hurried away from the tomb, afraid yet filled with joy, and ran to tell his disciples. Suddenly Jesus met them. "Greetings," | "Go and Tell." *he said. They came to him, clasped his feet and worshiped him. Then Jesus said to them, "Do not be afraid. Go and tell my brothers to go to Galilee; there they will see me."* ~ Matthew 28:1-10 NIV

"Go and Tell." Powerful words of Jesus. Words he said to a woman. Jesus could have risen from the dead and presented himself to one of his disciples, one of the Roman guards, or even a person walking by, but he chose to appear to Mary Magdalene.

This passage is significant because it shows that Jesus entrusted the important task of proclaiming the resurrection to women. In a society where women were often marginalized and not given the same rights and opportunities as men, Jesus chose to appear to a woman first and give her the task of spreading the good news.

> This passage is significant because it shows that Jesus entrusted the important task of proclaiming the resurrection to women.

Scholar James D. G. Dunn states that an account like this went against all cultural norms:

Mary holds the esteemed privilege of sharing news of the empty tomb with her fellow disciples. However, it's crucial to note that within the context of Middle Eastern society during that era, women were not often considered trustworthy witnesses. In legal proceedings, a woman's testimony held minimal weight. Furthermore, the fact that there were accounts of Mary previously being afflicted by demonic possession (Luke 8:2) would undoubtedly cast doubts on the credibility of any narrative linked to her, particularly in this case.[1]

The authenticity of this account shines through when we

consider the narrative choices. Had this been a concocted tale, the authors would likely have avoided relying on a woman's testimony, knowing the societal norms that devalued women as credible witnesses. Thus, the courage to present Mary's perspective stands as a testament to the story's integrity, enduring potential skepticism and incredulity. Yet, the account remained undeniably accurate, not because Mary happened to be the sole witness at the tomb, nor because there were no men available for the task. Instead, it was a deliberate, subversive, and radical choice to send Mary.

Throughout His earthly ministry, Jesus consistently shattered cultural barriers and exemplified the immense value and worth of women in society. He defied conventions, empowering women to step into active roles within the kingdom of God, transcending their traditional confines. By appointing them as co-laborers in His divine work, Jesus signaled a paradigm shift, ushering in a new era of inclusivity and equality.

As we read through the stories of women in the Bible, we see time and time again how they were emboldened by Jesus' teachings and example. Mary Magdalene's inclusion in the resurrection account serves as a poignant illustration of the pivotal role women assume in the narrative of salvation. This inclusion speaks to the heart of Jesus' radical message of love and equality transcending societal boundaries. The women depicted in the pages of the Bible were indeed emboldened by His influence.[2]

What Jesus did for Mary and for all women, in this scene is astounding. He told her to, *"Go quickly and tell His disciples" (Matthew 28:7 NIV).* Go and tell them that He lives. Go and tell them that Jesus is risen. Go and tell them there is hope in Jesus. Go and tell them.

And Jesus was telling me this too. Just like he told Mary not to be afraid, He was telling me that also. Just like he told Mary to *"go* and tell," He was telling me to go and pastor and preach and tell anyone who would listen that He lives.

This is a message spoken directly to your heart. God speaks to you as He did to Mary. His words resonate; "Go and tell them" (Matthew 28:10). The world is awaiting the Good News of His life-transforming presence.

> Go and tell them that He lives. Go and tell them that Jesus is risen. Go and tell them there is hope in Jesus. Go and tell them.

The enemy wants to silence the woman's voice, but Jesus has given us authority and grace to preach the Word of God. Be encouraged and empowered to use your gifts and talents to further the kingdom of God. Just like the women in Matthew 28, women today can boldly proclaim the good news of Jesus Christ and be used by God to impact the lives of those around them.

Ladies, let it be known, without a shadow of doubt, that your worth is not diminished because you are a woman. Do not entertain thoughts that question your significance or doubt your capability. Never believe for a moment that your voice lacks value. Remember, Mary Magdalene was graced by the favor of Jesus Christ, and that same favor extends to you. The hour has come to rise, to cast aside any lingering hesitations. It's a moment to conquer the fears that have held you captive. Embrace the call to action, and with unyielding determination, follow the directive to "Go and Tell."

Do Not Be Afraid

After this amazing time I had with the Lord, I felt emboldened, like Mary, to go and tell. To pastor the church with my husband and to say Yes to Jesus again, even when I was scared. I decided just to do it scared. Sometimes the insecurities and terror of stepping out

THE HOUR HAS COME TO RISE, TO CAST ASIDE ANY LINGERING HESITATIONS. IT'S A MOMENT TO CONQUER THE FEARS THAT HAVE HELD YOU CAPTIVE. EMBRACE THE CALL TO ACTION, AND WITH UNYIELDING DETERMINATION, FOLLOW THE DIRECTIVE TO "GO AND TELL.

into your calling never fades. Overcoming fear is remembering the 365 Bible verses that talk about not being afraid. If Moses and the Lord had to remind Joshua to be "*strong and courageous*" (Deuteronomy 31:7) I, too, need to be reminded.

As Moses prepared to pass the mantle of leadership to Joshua, he encouraged him to unleash his bravery. Taking on the responsibility of leading God's people can be daunting, but Joshua was made aware that the Lord was with him every step of the way. Frequently, when we encounter tasks that God has ordained for us that appear to be insurmountable and beyond our abilities, we may have a tendency to withdraw and feel inadequate and unworthy of fulfilling such significant roles and responsibilities.

"*Who am I,*" Moses said to God, "*that I should go to Pharaoh and bring the Israelites out of Egypt?*" (Exodus 3:11 NIV). Meg Bucher said it like this, "In every who am I moment, we can remember our I Am God."[3] He is the God who performs miracles, makes the impossible possible, created the world, and saves us. Because of His immense love for us, He includes us in His everlasting plan to ensure that everyone has an opportunity to hear the Gospel. In times when we may feel fearful of taking on the challenges and tasks that God has called us to, we can remember this truth that Moses said to the Israelites; "*Be strong and courageous. Do not be afraid or terrified because of them, for the Lord your God goes with you; he will never leave you or forsake you*" (Deuteronomy 31:6 NIV).

Following his speech to the Israelites, Moses shifted his focus to Joshua in particular:

Be strong and courageous, for you must go with these people into the land that the Lord swore to their ancestors to give them, and you must divide it among them as their inheritance. The Lord himself goes before you and will be with you; he will never leave you nor forsake you. Do not be afraid; do not be discouraged. ~ Deuteronomy 31:7-8 NIV

As the leader of the people, Joshua was expected to exhibit

strength and courage, both in his obedience to God's Word and in his perseverance through difficult circumstances. Joshua 1:9, emphasized the importance of being *"strong and courageous"* even in the face of endurance challenges. This was a pivotal moment for Joshua, likely causing him to feel anxious and apprehensive about the significant responsibility that lay ahead. However, they could confidently face their enemies with God's power on their side. God's encouragement stems from His loving and honest heart, reassuring us that He will never abandon us. We need not be afraid or disheartened.

> In a world of uncertainty and chaos, the unwavering nature of God is our beacon of hope,...

The reason we, along with Joshua, do not have to fear, has everything to do with who God is. In a world of uncertainty and chaos, the unwavering nature of God is our beacon of hope, eradicating all fear and doubt from our hearts and minds, just as it did for Joshua.

Joshua in the Old Testament found his confident steps rooted in his knowledge of God. Today, as New Testament believers, we have the assurance of God's presence within us through the indwelling of the Holy Spirit. Joshua found strength and courage as he obeyed the Lord's laws given through Moses, and we are also guided by God's commandments to keep us on a safe path. In the New Testament, Jesus teaches that, *"If you abide in me, and my words abide in you, ask for whatever you wish, and it will be done for you"* (John 15:7). Jesus, the Living Word of God, offers us the strength and courage we need to navigate life with confidence and purpose.

Repeatedly throughout the Bible, we see the phrase *"Be strong and courageous!"* used as a powerful message of encouragement from the Lord. Joshua was reminded of this several times, first by Moses and then directly by the Lord himself. This repetition of phraseology within the same passage of Scripture emphasizes its importance and highlights an essential attribute to look for in God's Word.

- *"Be strong and courageous, because you will lead these people to inherit the land I swore to their ancestors to give them,"* (Joshua 1:6 NIV).
- *"Be strong and very courageous. Be careful to obey all the law my servant Moses gave to you; do not turn from it to the right or to the left, that you may be successful wherever you go"* (Joshua 1:7 NIV).
- *"Have I not commanded you? Be strong and courageous. Do not be afraid; do not be discouraged, for the Lord your God will be with you wherever you go,"* (Joshua 1:9 NIV).
- *"Whoever rebels against your word and does not obey it, whatever you may command them, will be put to death. Only be strong and courageous!"* (Joshua 1:18 NIV).

God does not want us to be strong. God wants to be our strength.[4] Courage comes from the core of *who* He is and *whose* we are. Strength and courage come from a dedicated and obedient heart, through Christ. *"I'm a slave to Christ,"* Paul passionately wrote *(Titus 1:1)*. He knew he had to be, for every ounce of strength and courage Paul needed to face dire circumstances came from the Lord.[4]

> Fear didn't automatically leave, but if God told me to be strong, I would be. If God told me to be courageous, I knew He would be with me every step of the way, even if I was scared.

The moment I drew encouragement from Mary Magdalene, Moses, and Joshua, I was empowered and emboldened by the Spirit to first *"go and tell"* my husband that I was willing. Then to *"go and tell"* our church plant in Camaú. Fear didn't automatically leave, but if God told me to be strong, I would be. If God told me to be courageous, I knew He would be with me every step of the way, even if I was scared.

Seven years into co-pastoring Open Arms Church in Camalú, I can tell you that following the Spirit, stepping out of my comfort zone, and facing my insecurities was worth every moment. It is the joy of my life to pastor, to disciple, to teach, to lead Bible study, and to preach the Word of God. It has become my most favorite thing to do in ministry, and now, I get to preach at conferences, retreats, seminaries, and women's events all over the world.

What if fear stopped me? How many people wouldn't have heard the Word of God? How many people would never have heard the name of Jesus? I never want to be out of the will of God, that is horrifying. I want to continue to follow Him, to go all-in with His plans, and say yes to Jesus, even if I am afraid. Will you also go and tell, even if you are afraid?

Chapter 8
Tragedy, Loss, and Heart-Ache:
Fear of Not Being Enough

Courage doesn't always roar. Sometimes courage is the little voice at the end of the day that says I'll try again tomorrow.
~ Mary Anne Radmacher

THE YEAR WAS 2017, a mere twelve months after inaugurating our second campus in Camalú. I was granted a profound lesson in emulating Christ's love without fixating on outcomes. I learned to cherish the art of loving with an intensity that defied prior boundaries. The 150+ children, at two campuses, who were entrusted to our care emerged from fractured and vulnerable backgrounds, which accounted for their presence within our ministry. Amid this intricate mosaic, I discovered that loving them irrespective of the complexities—be it the mess, the sins, the shadows of the past, the aching wounds, the shattered pieces, the abyss of darkness, the trials of mental affliction, the burden of disabilities, the grasp of addiction, the single parent struggling with six, the widowed father, the orphans who lost both parents—embracing them all demanded resilience, and when all seemed to falter, we resolved to love yet again.

The Apostle Peter's counsel rang profoundly in my soul:
Above all, love each other deeply, because
love covers over a multitude of sins. ~ I Peter 4:8 NIV

Jesus' directive, also, echoed in our hearts— *"love one another as I have loved you"* (John 13:34). This nurturing from our Heavenly Father fortified Daniel and me, enabling us to extend compassion to *"the least of these"* (Matthew 25:40), emulating His boundless love for us. I don't always get this right. Loving your neighbor, loving those who have hurt you, or who have hurt others has been trying.

Through the conduit of these families and their stories, we have been granted an education on love of unparalleled value. We have learned from Sarah*[1] and her family that loving, even when complicated, is all worth it when God is glorified. Sarah's story is one of the most heart-rending accounts. With seven children and meager daily earnings from picking strawberries in the agricultural fields, she barely scrapes together the means to provide for her family.

Unbeknownst to her, her second husband had subjected her eldest daughter to a haunting ordeal of abuse since the tender age of fifteen. The revelation dawned when her daughter, at sixteen, became pregnant. With courage carved from desperation, she finally confessed the identity of the father—her stepfather. Sarah confronted a cultural conundrum. Such a scenario is distressingly commonplace in some corners of Mexico. She was entangled in a web of despair, cornered without reprieve. She called the police, but law enforcement proved ineffective despite her appeals. She was trapped. This vicious cycle persisted, with her daughter bearing another child by Sarah's husband shortly after Sarah herself gave birth to her last son.

Upon meeting them, I was awestruck by their resilience in the face of adversity. Initially, fury surged within me, aimed at a man I'd never met, a man who had caused unimaginable pain. I also grappled with animosity toward Sarah, the mother, for allowing this to happen under her roof, but amidst my turmoil, I heard the gentle whisper of God, urging me to embrace love beyond measure. I heard the Lord say, "Love them anyway."

"But God . . . ," I sighed, and He didn't let me finish my complaint to Him. Again He said, "Just love them."

So many times, deep down, you want to be the hero, rescue them, and bring them out of their situation. I have tried to do this too many times. But God was teaching me that only He could be the hero of their story. My job was just to love them and point them to Jesus. Alongside the steadfast Open Arms team, we chose to shower them with love, relinquishing their story to the hands of the One who transforms pain into redemption.

Love Looks Like Something

A resonating wisdom shared by missionary Heidi Baker, in Africa, echoes in my heart; "Love looks like something." It's in this spirit that we embraced Sarah and her family. We accepted both her children and her daughter's children into our childcare center, so they could continue to work to supply the basic needs of their families. We provided food, clothes, and prayers . . . lots of prayers for this family. We encouraged them to come to church and told them about Jesus. We were so excited when both mother and daughter accepted Him into their lives. Amid these efforts, we encouraged their escape from their dire situation, but they needed more than encouragement—they needed support. Fear paralyzed them from seeking help or escaping. We continued to pray for a solution and asked God to provide another place for them to live, so they could find peace and flee this abusive situation.

Several months after I prayed this prayer, Sarah came to me— her eyes glimmering with hope. She leaned in close and whispered to me that she had been saving money every month and had purchased a small piece of land. She was so proud of herself. She asked if we could help her move out so she could get on her own. She was being evicted. The people who loaned her the small, one-bedroom shack were coming back to claim it. My eyes lit up. "A blessing in disguise," I said to myself. This was her chance to get away from her abusive husband. This was her chance to have her own home. I gave her an overwhelming yes.

This was such a divine moment, because I actually needed to

talk to her about a blessing for her family. We had received a special donation that week, specifically to build a house for this family. The blessed pieces of Sarah's puzzle began to fall into place. She had the property, and Open Arms now had the funds to help build her a home. God was so good. He was writing their story right in front of our eyes. He knew exactly what they needed just when they needed it. What an amazing answer to prayer! This sounds like the perfect ending, and yes, it was perfectly planned by our Father—but fear, sin, and humanness got in the way.

Not the Happy Ending We Had Hoped For

Before we began the plans for their new home, we needed to determine how many bedrooms would fit in a house on their small lot. Sarah had seven children, and her daughter had two. As we sat down to talk to them both, her daughter Brenda[*2] decided that she wanted to start her own family and that this was her chance to be out on her own.

Brenda decided not to move in with her mom and her siblings; instead, she would find a place to move to with her stepdad, her abuser, and the father of her children. She was pregnant by him again. My heart shattered, and I prayed for a different solution. She thought this was her best option. We quickly came up with another solution so we could help her escape this situation. My husband came up with a plan to build a duplex on her mom's property so she could have her own home also. Yet again, Brenda didn't affirm this option. My heart grieved. My mind couldn't comprehend. Was this the only "love" she had ever received? I went to her. I talked and pleaded, and I prayed and hoped for another solution. I could understand not wanting to live with your mom your whole life, but I couldn't fathom her decision of moving in with her stepdad.

I again pleaded with her and even offered to rent a place for her and her children. I even went around town looking for a room for her to rent. In the end, she chose not to receive our help. She may possibly have experienced the Stockholm Syndrome, in which because of the human desire to survive, a victim acclimates themselves to an abusive situation so much so that they say to other people that they are okay.

I wish I could tell you this story had a different ending. We love to write and tell about all the amazing things that happen on the mission field, because God is absolutely amazing. But it is difficult to share with you about our failures, or the outcomes that are the opposite of what we had prayed for. It wouldn't be honest, though, if I didn't share some of the hardships, hurts, and hurdles.

I cried out to God many nights for Brenda and her children. I thanked Him for the brand new home for Sarah and her kids, but my heart grieved for Brenda; "God, isn't there another way? God, please help. God, we need a miracle here." He just whispered, "Love her."

Moments where my capacity falters and my toolbox of solutions feels inadequate.

I've come to understand that I can't mend every broken thread. The fabric of my nature is woven with an affinity to repair, to find solutions, and to get things done. My heart finds its rhythm in action, in the very act of service and solving problems. Yet, there are instances that defy my skills. Moments where my capacity falters and my toolbox of solutions feels inadequate. In these instances, a humbling awareness settles in, a realization that even my best efforts can't mend all fractures. This truth stands resolute—there are knots too complex for me to untangle, and it's in this realization that a

...even my best efforts can't mend all fractures.

sense of inadequacy unfurls. The fear of failure, of letting down this family, letting down God, and falling short of my calling—all surge forth like a raging storm. The gusts of this fear threaten to overturn my sense of purpose, to drown me in a sea of doubt.

I knew how to swim, but the wind and the waves of this fear were too strong for me. I grieved my limitations and weaknesses. The hurricane of fear and the relentless waves of doubt could only be calmed by surrender. Surrendering this family to my Jesus was difficult. To be honest, I feel like I failed this family, and I still struggle with the outcome today.

Every time I gaze into the eyes of Brenda's children, my heart swells with a mix of emotions. Their innocence, their resilience, and their future stand before me, a canvas awaiting the masterstroke. Yet, the brush isn't mine to wield. Their narrative isn't mine to script. I'm but a vessel, a witness to their unfolding story. I had to have *"hope as an anchor for the soul, firm and secure"* (Hebrews 6:19). I know that the plans Jesus has for her are that she would *"always have a hope and a future"* (Jeremiah 29:11).

Through Sarah and Brenda, I've gleaned profound lessons in love and courage. I feared that I was not enough for them or their situation. However, their lives have etched in me the art of loving relentlessly, even when it hurts your soul. They've shown me that love transcends outcomes and that I am not the hero, but Jesus is. Their presence in my life has taught me to stand bravely in the face of uncertainty and to embrace vulnerability. In their journey, I've discovered the beauty of loving until it hurts, and even when it hurts. They have taught me the true meaning of 1 Corinthians 13:7 NLT:

> *Love never gives up, never loses faith, is always hopeful, and endures through every circumstance.*

...I am not the hero, but Jesus is.

They have illuminated the path to a love that perseveres, a love that hopes for redemption in its fullest form. In the shadow of their lives, I've found my own courage—courage to anchor myself to the true Anchor, and to let Him navigate the storms and the winds. He is my compass, and He is ultimately in control.

The True Mark of Courage Is Not in Never Falling Down

I talk about the importance of being courageous in the face of fear. But sometimes, when we're scared and uncertain, summoning that kind of bravery can feel impossible. That's when we need to remember that courage doesn't always come as a mighty roar. Sometimes, the quiet voice inside us says, "say yes, even if you are afraid" [4]   And that is being brave.

It's so easy to get discouraged when we fail or fall short. Have you attempted to positively change your life or the lives of others but have stumbled along the way? Let me encourage you. The true mark of courage is not in never falling down, but in getting back up and trying again, even when it's difficult. If we learn to be brave in small ways, we can build up the strength and confidence to face more enormous challenges with faith and resilience. So many of us have been taught that courage is loud and dramatic. We picture a warrior charging fearlessly into battle or a hero risking life and limb to save the day, but courage often looks much quieter and less glamorous than that. Sometimes courage is simply getting up daily and facing our fears, even when we're trembling with worry.

> Courage doesn't always come as a mighty roar. Sometimes, the quiet voice inside us says, "say yes, even if you are afraid" And that is being brave.

Most often your bravery won't make headlines or win medals. The actual test of courage is whether we're willing to keep trying, even when we are afraid, unsure, or grieving. This means taking small steps toward our goals, even when the path ahead seems daunting. It signifies reaching out for help when we need it, even if we feel embarrassed or vulnerable. It represents learning to forgive ourselves when we stumble or fall short, so that we can pick ourselves up and try again. Even when we feel like giving up, remember what David tells us in Psalm 23:4 NIV:

> Even though I walk
> > through the darkest valley,
> I will fear no evil,
> > for you are with me;
> your rod and your staff,
> > they comfort me.

I am grateful for God's comfort, even during the most brutal trials. Being on the mission field is not glamorous, easy, or without pain and grief. I could write more on miracles, provision, and fruit, but I would only tell you part of the story. The reality of missions is that sometimes, even when you have given your all, prayed, fasted, and yearned for God to make a way, He doesn't always write the story that you ask for. I know He is not done writing Sarah and Brenda's stories. I have learned that when things aren't good yet, it is because God is not finished. I hope for change, and I stay lion-hearted even if I don't have the loudest roar. I have learned that I don't have to roar the most vociferously to be courageous. I hope for freedom for

I have learned that when things aren't good yet, it is because God is not finished.

this family. I will continue to love them, despite it all, because I John 4:8 NIV is clear; "Whoever does not love does not know God, because God is love." Let's learn to love, despite the outcome, because God is love, and let's continue to be brave even when valor doesn't look like we think it should.

Some years have been more challenging than others. We have overwhelming testimonies about God's goodness, but some years, we have had some hard losses. To be honest, I would rather talk about all the wins—all the children off the streets and out of orphanages, all the children able to grow up with their families—because all children belong with families. I would rather talk about all the moms, dads, youth, and kids who have come to know the Lord, and were baptized. I love talking about this, and we should because it glorifies God, but I have also learned to find Jesus in pain, loss, and death.

I Am Not Enough

In this world, problems come in various shades, but then there are those classified as third-world problems. In our ministry here in Mexico, amid some of the most economically disadvantaged and vulnerable families, we've witnessed immense pain, loss, and tragedy. The shadows of death loom larger than I ever anticipated, a stark reminder of the fragility of life. We've found ourselves presiding over as many funerals as weddings and celebrating births as often as mourning deaths. The cycle of life persists, but it remains heart wrenchingly challenging. Words often fail to soothe grief, and the most fitting Bible verse can escape my memory in the moment of need. In these times, I recognize my own insufficiency. In these times, I fear that I fail more people than I can help and that I will never be enough.

> ...I fear that I fail more people than I can help and that I will never be enough.

I am not enough. Only Christ's sufficiency is enough.

Sometimes, just being there, extending a hand, and offering love to those in pain, is comforting enough. It's a fragile hope that we clasp onto—our prayers inter-mingling with our hopes—that Jesus' all-sufficient grace prevails, al-ways.

We Have a Lot of Wins, but We Also Have Losses

Enrique and Ezra*[5] endured the heartache of losing their father to an incurable illness. Just under a year later, tragedy struck again, stealing away their mother in a heartbreaking automobile accident. They became true orphans, shouldering a burden of profound loss. Regrettably, this story of loss isn't unique among the children we care for. Too many times, I have had to sit with some of the children and tell them that their father lost his battle with cancer, that their mom didn't make it out of surgery, or that their father was being sent to jail.

> I am not enough. Only Christ's sufficiency is enough.

Sometimes I get the job no one would ever want. Many times, when tragedy strikes, the families want me to give their children the bad news. This shows their deep trust in me, which is a blessing, however, the right words evade me far too often. Within the heart-wrenching tapestry of these stories, the story of Enrique and Ezra left me speechless. These boys have now lost both of their parents, and I vowed they would not be taken to an orphanage. I could feel my heart harden-ing. I found myself grappling with questions directed to God, won-dering aloud, "Is this Your plan, God? Haven't they endured enough? Surely, there must be a more merciful path. Wouldn't you be more glorified through healing their dad, or through saving their mother from tragedy?" I'm cognizant of God's sovereignty, His sight beyond the limits of my own vision, yet, as I walked alongside these boys through yet another loss, the weight of it all felt almost unbearable.

The harsh currents of tragedy have tested my capacity for

compassion. I've strived to maintain an open heart, even amid adversity, even when mistreated or scarred by the cruel edges of sin. Yet, the pain of losing another mother, another cherished friend, surpassed my emotional armor. Witnessing our staff gather around these boys, offering solace through shared meals, genuine care, and fervent prayers, touched me profoundly. They exhibited a depth of love that persisted even through darkness, fear, uncertainty, and the raw unfairness of life's twists and turns. The resilient Mexican spirit has taught me lessons money could never buy.

Another Tragedy

Just a mere few months after the heartache of losing Enrique and Ezra's mother, we were struck again with another heartwrenching blow as we mourned the loss of Raquel.[6] At just twenty one-years-old, this young mother's life took a tragic turn when her brakes failed, forcing her to make a fateful choice. She leapt from her moving car, opting to face injury or death rather than collide with a solid wall. This decision left her husband and their one-year-old baby girl, whose first birthday aligned tragically with the day of her mother's funeral, behind in a wake of sorrow. Describing our emotions with the news of this loss seems inadequate. Devastation for this family feels like an understatement. I began to wonder if the weight of further tragedies was something I could bear. Amidst this turmoil, a resounding phrase echoed through my thoughts, a divine whisper from heaven; "In death, there will be life." I clung to these words, repeating this promise to the grieving families time and time again. Just as Jesus had offered solace to Mary and Martha in the face of Lazarus' passing, so I too held onto the hope that life could emerge from the depths of loss.

Jesus told her, I am the resurrection and the life. Anyone who believes in me will live, even after dying. Everyone who lives in me and

believes in me will never ever die. Do you believe this, Martha? ~ John
11:25-26 NLT

Did I Believe This?

I did believe, although the ache within me refused to wane.
Nonetheless, we bore witness to the unfaltering validation of His
promises. In the wake of Raquel's death, an unforeseen sequence
of events unfolded—her husband, shattered by grief, found solace
accepting the Lord as His Savior. Her mother-in-law, too, was
touched by the grace of Jesus. Her heart transformed. Even their
neighbor, touched by the ripples of faith radiating from this tragic
loss, embraced the gospel's message. From the shadows of death,
life emerged. Not mere earthly exis-
tence, but the promise of eternal life. In
the midst of it all, Jesus always wins—
His faithfulness, an enduring constant.
In the words penned by Apostle Paul in
Philippians 1:21 NIV, the truth resounds, "For to me, to live is Christ
and to die is gain."

> In the midst of it all,
> Jesus always wins...

And Yet, More Losses

Two weeks later, tragedy struck again within our community.
One of the members of High Voltage, our vibrant youth group, endured a heart-wrenching loss—both her brother and father were
taken from her by a drunken driver on the highway. The location of
the nearest hospital, equipped to provide adequate care is a two-
hour journey away, a seemingly insurmountable distance when every
minute is crucial. In the face of this overwhelming sorrow, words
seemed inadequate. Instead, I embraced the young sister and daughter, offering a comforting hug and a space for her tears to flow.

I cried too, echoing the anguish that enveloped us all.

I've witnessed the incredible strength of spirit-filled women of God who've walked into a hospital with the anticipation of delivering their child, only to leave without their baby, the child having passed away within their womb. I've stood beside a mother, her baby born prematurely via C-section, only for her to be hurriedly discharged within twenty four hours, the hospital bed urgently needed for another expectant mother. Yet, fate dealt her a cruel hand, propelling her back to the hospital during the night, now suffering with a blood clot in her lung. While in the hospital she stopped breathing, and she went into cardiac arrest, the toll of it all left her with severe brain damage. It was then, within those critical moments, that my privilege was underscored—nurturing her premature infant through breastfeeding, a connection I treasured as if the child were my own. I was able to give life and sustenance to her baby, while she was being treated in the ICU. I loved that baby like my own, and just as much as I cared for her two other children. I knelt in prayer, seeking the miraculous restoration of their mother's health.

After several months in intensive care, she was finally discharged. Due to her brain damage, it became evident that her journey would require ongoing, round-the-clock care, an immense responsibility shouldered by her dedicated husband. Open Arms staff and donors rallied around him, offering unwavering support in the face of adversity. However, the story took an unfortunate turn a year later, as she passed away, leaving us all heartbroken and reeling from the loss. My prayers, along with those of everyone who knew her, resounded fervently for a miracle that wasn't meant to be.

I am friends with a mother who faced the agonizing reality of having nothing to offer her hungry children. She resorted to scavenging through the garbage, and once, in dire desperation, even breaking into her neighbors' home to secure a few tortillas. Glimpses of suffering are evident. The voice of the enemy would try to taunt me by questioning God's goodness. Nonetheless, my unshakable belief remains that God stands as an unwavering, benevolent Father. I would repeat verses in Psalms aloud when Satan's lies invaded my thoughts.

Oh, taste and see that the Lord is good!
Blessed is the man who takes refuge in him! ~ Psalms 34:8 NIV
Or this verse:
Give thanks to the Lord, for he is good,
for his steadfast love endures forever! ~ Psalms 107:1 ESV

Amidst the shadows of loss, tragedy, and pain, I've embarked on a profound journey of discovering His presence and knowing without a doubt that He is good.

Through the most heartrending circumstances, He has imparted the wisdom to seek Him, unveiling His provision and unfathomable beauty amidst the lives of those burdened by distress, loss, and mourning.

In his Sermon on the Mount, Jesus said:
Blessed are those who mourn for they shall be comforted.
~ Matthew 5:4 ESV

He is my Comforter. Without my Comforter, the Holy Spirit, I would not have been able to continue fighting the good fight. Friends, lean into Him. Death is not the end, not in the light of eternity. We must be steadfast to remember that our fight is not for this life, but for eternity.

> Death is not the end, not in the light of eternity. We must be steadfast to remember that our fight is not for this life, but for eternity.

Truly, truly, I say to you, he who hears My word, and believes Him who sent Me, has eternal life, and does not come into judgment, but has passed out of death into life. ~ John 5:24 NASB

AMIDST THE SHADOWS OF LOSS, TRAGEDY, AND PAIN, I'VE EMBARKED ON A PROFOUND JOURNEY OF DISCOVERING HIS PRESENCE AND KNOWING WITHOUT A DOUBT THAT HE IS GOOD.

Anchored in Hope

We press on. We press on in love. We persist in hope. We prevail in our fight, so that every individual, every child, every family may encounter the profound hope that only Jesus brings, even in this fractured world. Through my journey, I've come to anchor my hope solely in Jesus.

Death, a constant echo, keeps reminding us that we reside in a world marred by brokenness. It's a constant whisper of our mortality, a reminder that our days here are finite, and that our bodies will ultimately return to the earth. I am reminded by this truth.

> Our hope is anchored in Jesus Christ, who has gone before us and conquered sin and death.

But we are citizens of heaven, where the Lord Jesus Christ lives.

And we are eagerly waiting for him to return as our Savior.

He will take our weak mortal bodies and change them into glorious bodies like his own, using the same power with which he will bring everything under his control.
~ Philippians 3:20-21 NLT

As we await this glorious day, there is an unyielding glimmer of hope. I want to remind you of our hope in Jesus Christ, which transcends this world and all its difficulties.

In Hebrews 6:18-19 NLT, we read:
So God has given both his promise and his oath.
These two things are unchangeable
because it is impossible for God to lie.
Therefore, we who have fled to him for refuge can have
great confidence as we hold to the hope that lies before us.
This hope is a strong and trustworthy anchor for our souls.
It leads us through the curtain into God's inner sanctuary.
What does this mean for us in the midst of our pain and sorrow?

First, it means that we have a secure hope anchored in someone greater than ourselves, someone greater than this world. Our hope is anchored in Jesus Christ, who has gone before us and conquered sin and death.

This hope is not wishful thinking or mere optimism. On the contrary, it is a hope grounded in God's promises. As the writer of Hebrews says, *"So God has given both his promise and his oath. These two things are unchangeable because it is impossible for God to lie. Therefore, we who have fled to him for refuge can have great confidence as we hold to the hope that lies before us"* (Hebrews 6:18).

Friends, maybe you have gone through a heartache, tragedy, loss, or death also. Remember to anchor your hope in Jesus, even amid your fears and most challenging, painful, and trying times. Together, let's secure our souls in Jesus Christ, who has gone before us and has prepared a place for us in the presence of God. I want to encourage you, just as I remind myself, our hope is not anchored in the confines of this world. Instead, it finds its foundation in the One who conquered death and will ultimately return for those who believe. Let's remember what Revelation 21:4 NIV tells us, *"He will wipe every tear from their eyes. There will be no more death or mourning or crying or pain, for the old order of things has passed away."*

> Don't grow weary of doing good, even when it hurts.

Until this day, dear friends, let hope in Jesus be your anchor during the ugliest of storms. Keep going. Keep up the good fight. Don't grow weary of doing good, even when it hurts. Always when it hurts. This is being brave. You are brave.

Chapter 9
If It's Not Good, God's Not Done:
Fear of Failure

A hero is no braver than an ordinary man, but he is brave five minutes longer. ~ Ralph Waldo Emerson.

IN 2018, a lovely couple came into our office in Camalú eager to tell us their story, desperate for help and a sign that God was still with them. Notably nervous, they began to share their heart-wrenching story of when they lived in Tijuana in 2004. (In 2004, Daniel and I were working at the orphanage, Rancho de Sus Niños, before we began Open Arms. And this couple lived near that orphanage, but we did not know them.) With palpable unease, the gentleman began to recount the heart-wrenching events that unfolded in Tijuana back in 2004. He said, "It was a normal day of work. Our two daughters didn't have school that day, so as we left for work, we locked the doors of our home, to make sure no one could get in. We went about our day, until I got a phone call that our house was on fire. We rushed home to find our house in ashes, and to the worst news someone could receive; our daughters had burned to death."

As his words hung in the air, the weight of their sorrow bore down on the room, leaving me utterly stunned. My eyes widened, my mouth ajar in disbelief. Emotions surged, and tears welled up uncontrollably. In unison, we wept as their agonizing memories unfolded, each tear a testament to the pain they carried. In the midst of this raw and harrowing account, my thoughts oscillated between the recollection of a similar tragedy we read of in the newspaper during our orphanage days in Tecate, in 2004. Could this possibly be the same couple? Was this their story that had remained etched in our hearts? Fourteen years later, the question persisted as they sat before us, courageously revisiting their anguish.

Extracting a newspaper clipping from their belongings, the weight of déjà vu bore down. My heart seemed to plummet, mirroring the depth of despair embedded within that ill-fated story. This was the same story we had recounted to visiting mission teams and this story was one of the reasons we decided to start Open Arms. Astonishingly, the couple who had endured this tragedy was now seated before us, once again seeking solace. The sorrow that had pierced our hearts years ago was resurfacing in the present moment. The odds of this convergence felt astronomical—the encounter of these two paths, separated by time and circumstance, within the confines of our small rural town of Camalú. Only God could have put us together eighteen years later.

The unspoken question hung in the air, a question we all grappled with: What was God doing? What were the odds of this couple finding us in the small rural town of Camalú? What was God trying to tell us now? What was God up to?

The couple shared how they had heard about our ministry's positive impact on families, particularly our commitment to ensuring children were not locked in their homes while their parents worked. They revealed that it had always been their dream to establish a ministry akin to ours. I was in shock by their words. They continued to tell us that, due to lack of support, they had recently shut the doors of their small church that they had on their property. They were desperate for someone to help them. They had never stopped dreaming of creating a childcare center on their 16,000 square foot property in the dusty farming town of Los Pinos, an hour south of Camalú, in the San Quintin Valley of Baja California.

Their journey had led them to knock on many doors, seeking assistance. They said that our door was the last door they were going to knock on and ask for help. They were ready to give up. As they continued to share their story and their vision for their property, they humbly implored us to share our wisdom and experience, and to mentor them as they sought to turn their dream into reality. Without hesitation, we responded with an emphatic "YES!" We would help anyone who's vision aligned with Open Arms. A kinship took root, intertwining our lives with theirs, as my husband Daniel and I took on the role of mentors to this couple.

Through a series of discussions, it became clear that they faced significant challenges. They lacked resources and a dedicated team, yet their determination burned bright, fueled by a fervent desire to spare other families from the gut-wrenching tragedy that they had endured. As the mentorship evolved, a pivotal decision emerged from their depths—the couple chose to donate their property to Open Arms.

The sheer magnitude of their gesture left us humbled, astonished, and profoundly grateful. We pledged to prayerfully consider this unexpected turn of events, engaging our Board of Directors to discern if this was God's will for our ministry. Our plate was already overflowing, having recently established our Camalú campus and undertaking the construction of a mission team dormitory. Despite the weight of our existing commitments, we also recognized the uncanny alignment of circumstances. What were the chances that this couple, whose story we had recounted countless times to underscore our mission's purpose, would cross our path in such an unforeseen manner? Only God.

A Literal Sign

This wonderful couple had invited us out to see their property as we were in discussion about the donation. It was a one-hour drive from our campus in Camalú. I took advantage of the drive and prayed for clarity and confirmation. My prayer went something like this, "God this sounds like a good idea, but if this isn't your idea, I don't want any part in it. If this is what you want us to do, where you want us to go, if you want us to open our arms again, I need you to confirm this in a tangible way. Give me a sign that this is the direction to go."

I felt like Gideon again, but I wanted God to be clear with me. I remember Moses asking God for confirmation that God would go with him as they headed to the Promised Land in Exodus 33:12-18. Here I was, again, afraid to proceed if God didn't go before me. Remember, my biggest fear is being out of the will of God, and that fear surged once again.

As we arrived at the property, I stepped out of the car and cast my gaze across the dirt road. A laugh escaped me—God's sense of humor, it seemed, was in full play. In a surreal twist, a small-scale convenience store stood before me emblazoned with my name, "Abarrotes Heidi." My name was an unusual one in Mexico, and was usually spelled differently, but this store name was spelled precisely as I spelled mine. Yet, the astonishment didn't stop there; to my left stood "Ferreteria Danny," Danny's Hardware Store. It was beyond belief—our names adorning signs, side by side, in front of the Los Pinos property. A peculiar coincidence? Perhaps not.

I shared this surreal encounter with my mother, seeking her perspective. Her response was unequivocal: "Heidi, what more confirmation do you need?" Indeed, God had responded to my prayer in a way that could not be ignored—an affirmation quite literally written in the names of the stores before us. The sign was unmistakable; God had communicated His approval for the next chapter of Open Arms through the signs that bore our names. With excitement, trepidation, and of course some fear, we embraced this new God-ordained adventure. After all, true impact rarely emerges from the comfort zone, does it?

The community of Los Pinos, while smaller than Camalú, shares similarities in its plight. It's a place where the urgent need for a child-care center is undeniable. Here, parents work relentlessly in the agricultural fields, dedicating twelve grueling hours to the soil from dawn till dusk, earning meager wages as low as fifteen dollars a day. Yet, these sparse earnings don't afford them the luxury of paying for childcare, forcing many to grapple with a heart-wrenching dilemma. Children are often left in their homes in the care of "older" siblings, some as young as six years old. These young children, who are supposed to be in school, are now stuck at home, handling responsibilities beyond their age. Their innocence is overshadowed by the weight of the duties, and this vulnerable situation occurs in an uncertain environment without a safe space for them to grow while their parents work tirelessly.

Our conviction remains unwavering—every child within our reach deserves the chance to attend school, to feel safe, to remain with their families, and to be introduced to the love of Jesus. Our encounter with this couple felt like more than mere coincidence. It bore the mark of divine orchestration. Fueled by this conviction, we embraced God's unfolding plan with a resounding yes once more, even though it was scary.

The year 2018 drew to a close with a pivotal announcement—the prospect of our third campus in Los Pinos. The subsequent year, 2019, became a year of focus and determination. We directed our energies towards completing the dormitories in Camalú while rallying resources for the inaugural phase of our Los Pinos campus. Amid these efforts, a defining moment transpired—the legal papers that designated the property as Open Arms were signed, solidifying our commitment to this new endeavor.

Then, as the dawn of 2020 arrived, so did an unforeseen global upheaval—the Covid-19 pandemic. In its wake, construction permits were elusive, temporarily stalling the commencement of our building efforts. Instead, we focused on completing the construction of the off-campus house we were building for the couple who so graciously donated their land to Open Arms.

Wait Patiently for the Lord

During this period, an unfortunate rupture emerged between this couple and our primary contractor, casting a shadow of uncertainty over the Open Arms project. The news hit us like a tidal wave of sorrow, leaving us reeling from the unexpected blow. We fervently sought avenues for reconciliation, but the prospects appeared bleak and remote. Amidst these turbulent waters, an additional layer of complexity emerged—the couple decided not to move into the house we were constructing for them off the property, due to this disagreement. In order for us to build the childcare center, and church plant, the old house on the property needed to be demolished, but this was their current home.

In Mexico, a legal provision grants certain rights to individuals who reside on a property, even if they are not the property's owners. This backdrop introduced an option for legal recourse, one that could have been pursued through court proceedings—an avenue that would likely have been decided in our favor. However, we harbored a deep-seated conviction to uphold the honor of their story and to mend the wounds inflicted by the tragic loss of their daughters in that devastating house fire.

> With the weight of uncertainty resting upon us, we chose patience over haste, faith over fear, and prayerful anticipation over rash action.

Amidst the tumult, we engaged in candid conversations with our board members and on-ground leaders, seeking collective wisdom and divine guidance. In unity, we arrived at a resolute decision—to surrender to the power of prayer and place our trust in the hands of the Lord. With the weight of uncertainty resting upon us, we chose patience over haste, faith over fear, and prayerful anticipation over rash action. These words of the Psalmist were what kept my faith alive during this trying time.

Yet I am confident I will see the Lord's goodness
while I am here in the land of the living.
Wait patiently for the Lord.
Be brave and courageous.
Yes, wait patiently for the Lord. ~ Psalm 27:13-14, NLT

As Christians, there will be times in our lives when we are faced with obstacles that seem insurmountable. This was one of the hardest seasons I ever had to endure. It was easy to become discouraged and lose hope when we didn't see any immediate solutions to our problems. However, Psalm 27:13-14 reminded me that even in the midst of my struggles, I could be confident in the Lord's goodness.

This is a reminder that the Lord is always working for our good, even when we can't see it. We can trust that His plans for us are good (Jeremiah 29:11), and that He will come through for us in His perfect timing.

Waiting on the Lord can be difficult, especially when we feel like we're in the midst of a battle. Doubt, and fear can creep in, like a thief in the night. That's why Psalm 27:14 encourages us to be brave and courageous as we wait patiently for the Lord. This verse is a call to action. It is a reminder that we need to actively trust in the Lord and rely on His strength during our times of waiting.

So, if you're in a season of waiting, take heart. Remember that the Lord is with you, and He will never leave you or forsake you (Deuteronomy 31:8 NIV). Be brave and courageous as you wait patiently for Him to move in your situation. Above all, trust in His goodness and His perfect timing, knowing that He is always working for your good.

God never wastes a waiting season. Every waiting season is a preparation period if you wait patiently on the Lord. Remember, "if it's not good yet, God's not done."[1]

If It's Not Good Yet, God's Not Done

In the midst of this season of waiting, we found ourselves immersed in a profound period of mourning. We grieved not only for
the vision of a future child care center that could care for seventy
five vulnerable children, but also for the potential church plant that
held the promise of transform-
ing lives for the glory of God.

In the midst of this journey,
I was drawn to the narrative recounted in John 11:1-45—the
poignant account of Lazarus's
resurrection by Jesus. It is a tale
of supplication, delayed re-

> God never wastes a wait-
> ing season. Every waiting
> season is a preparation pe-
> riod if you wait patiently
> on the Lord.

sponse, and miraculous intervention. Mary and Martha, begged Jesus
to intercede for their gravely ill brother. They were met with silence
and a period of waiting. It wasn't until Lazarus had succumbed to
death that Jesus chose to act. In this story, a profound truth
emerged. Jesus declared, "This sickness will not end in death. No, it
is for God's glory so that God's Son may be glorified through it"
(John 11:4 NIV). In the case of Lazarus, as well as in the saga of the
Los Pinos campus, a common thread emerged. God sought to manifest His glory.

Despite the seeming darkness that clouded the moment, and
the disheartening appearance of a dream deferred, I found solace
in believing that God's timing held the key. The situation may have
lacked an immediate manifestation of His glory, yet I remained steadfast in the belief that God's ultimate purpose would be fulfilled. My
aspiration was not to echo Martha's complaints, but to emulate
Mary's posture of worship. Thus, I humbled myself, taking to my
knees in prayer and fasting. In an act reminiscent of our earlier surrender of our last dollar to God sixteen years prior, I relinquished

this cherished dream back into His capable hands. Just as in times past, this act of surrender became an act of faith, a declaration that I trusted His timing and that, ultimately, God's glory would shine forth.

During this time, God reminded me that His delay was not denial. Let's continue to look at this Scripture passage in John:

Now Jesus loved Martha and her sister and Lazarus.

So when he heard that Lazarus was sick, he stayed where he was two more days, and then he said to his disciples, "Let us go back to Judea."

On his arrival, Jesus found that Lazarus had already been in the tomb for four days. ~ John 11:5-7, 17 NIV

Jesus waited two days to act after the news reached Him. When He arrived in Bethany where Martha, Mary, and Lazarus were, Lazarus had already been dead for four days.

The delay was not a denial, and Jesus is always on time. He is faithful to fulfill His promises to us. He is so faithful that He will let something die in us in order for us to experience the power of His resurrection.

> The delay was not a denial, and Jesus is always on time.

Jesus delayed going to visit Lazarus, even knowing that he was sick. Jesus knew that Lazarus had to die in order to manifest his power so that people would believe in him.

After contemplating this story, God was telling me that there was nothing too dead for Him. We serve a God who can resurrect someone who has been dead for four days, and I held the faith that God would resurrect the Los Pinos campus. I believed that there is nothing too dead for God.

When I read this story, I always wonder why he waited so long. Why didn't he come back earlier? It wasn't that far—just three kilometers.

You know why? So, no one would get the credit for what was going to happen.

Lazarus died, the wake and the funeral passed. No minister could receive the credit. No person could bear the glory of what was to happen. Jesus delayed his return so all the glory would be His.

He was teaching me through this season, and this story, that something has to die, for it to receive resurrection power. I sensed God was telling me that this campus will not end in death, but the wait was so that Jesus would be glorified.

The Los Pinos endeavor had deteriorated to a state of dormancy for a full year. Then, in May of 2021, a pivotal call reached us— the donating couple expressed an intention to leave the property so we could begin construction. A true miracle. The resurrection of a dream.

In my heart, I held unwavering faith that this property had been set apart for Open Arms.

> When you find yourself traversing a season of waiting, where your aspirations appear lifeless and decomposing, remember this truth: If it's not good yet, God's not done.

The signs, undeniable and conspicuous, formed an unambiguous confirmation. In our plea for a sign, God responded by adorning the two store signs directly in front of the property with our very names.

Through seasons of patient waiting and resolute faith, even when the dream appeared lifeless and beyond salvaging, God breathed new life into it—a parallel reminiscent of the resurrection of Lazarus.

Lynn Winters, a dear friend and Pastor, aptly encapsulated this concept during a sermon at our Camalú church. He proclaimed, "If it's not good yet, God's not done." This declaration became my anthem, and it's a sentiment that can resonate within your heart as well. When you find yourself traversing a season of waiting, where your aspirations appear lifeless and decomposing, remember this truth: If it's not good yet, God's not done.

Miraculously, possession of the Los Pinos land was secured, and a momentous occasion unfolded on July 20th, 2021—the official groundbreaking. Throughout this journey, the refrain resounded continually—God is faithful, and His timing is perfect. His constancy never wavers (Revelation 1:18), and His promises stand resolute, affirmed with a resounding "Yes" and "Amen" (2 Corinthians 1:20). We have borne witness to His faithfulness anew, witnessing His mighty hand at work once more.

Resurrection Miracle

Yet, if I were to be honest, I must confess that throughout that year of waiting, I grappled with a profound sense of inadequacy. I felt like I failed. The weight of failure was a heavy burden, an unrelenting concern that I had disappointed not only our faithful supporters, but also our dedicated staff and the future generations of children who would have eventually run the halls of the envisioned childcare center. Amidst the shadows of uncertainty, fear took root, whispering doubts that perhaps God would not uphold His promise as assuredly as I had believed. In those moments, my faith wavered—a stark reminder of my own frailty. However, let me stand as a testament before you: God remains unwaveringly the God of miracles. Just when His presence appears concealed, just as it seems time has slipped away, just when circumstances mirror the lifelessness of the tomb, therein lies the perfect breeding ground for God's awe-inspiring resurrection miracle.

As I write this, we are ninety percent finished with the construction at the Los Pinos campus. Although the church building wasn't built yet, I started hosting a ladies Bible study there as soon as we took possession of the property in 2021. I started it with twelve women, underneath the tree in the center of the property. That was our humble beginnings. Three years later, it has grown to more than one hundred women, thirty five men, and tons of children that come every Thursday. Remarkably, even before the church was formally established and the childcare facility inaugurated, hundreds have found salvation in Jesus through our gatherings. What the enemy meant for evil God has used to bring himself glory. I think failure in man's eyes is completely different from God's viewpoint. Fear of failure immobilizes many, thwarting them from even taking that first step. But let me urge you—God's perspective defies these limitations. Don't let fear deter you from embracing that leap of faith; don't let fear inhibit you from unleashing your bravery.

Conquering Your Fear of Failure

It's important to remember that our fear of failure often stems from a desire for the approval and acceptance of others. The Bible acknowledges this human tendency and guides us toward a more profound understanding of where our true worth lies. Galatians 1:10 NLT reminds us:

Obviously, I'm not trying to win the approval of people, but of God. If pleasing people were my goal, I would not be Christ's servant.

As followers of Christ, we are called to prioritize God's opinion above all else. Our worth is rooted in His love and acceptance, not in the fleeting judgments of people.

Even when we fall short in the eyes of man, we can rest assured that God's love for us is unwavering and unconditional. Romans 8:38-39 NIV assures us:

For I am convinced that neither death nor life, neither angels nor demons, neither the present nor the future, nor any powers, neither height nor

> As followers of Christ, we are called to prioritize God's opinion above all else.

depth, nor anything else in all creation, will be able to separate us from the love of God that is in Christ Jesus our Lord.

Such a profound truth reminds us that our failures don't diminish God's unending affection for us. We are called to trust in God's plan and purpose for our lives, even when it doesn't align with our own expectations. Jeremiah 17:7-8 NIV encapsulates this sentiment:

But blessed is the one who trusts in the LORD, whose confidence is in him.

They will be like a tree planted by the water that sends out its roots by the stream. It does not fear when heat comes; its leaves are always green. It has no worries in a year of drought and never fails to bear fruit.

While our human understanding may breed fear of failure, relinquishing our plans to God ensures a path illuminated by His wisdom.

Let me encourage you. Don't be captivated by your fear of failure. Instead, trust in God's perfect plan for your life and step out in faith, knowing that your successes and failures are ultimately in His hands. Remember, "if it is not good yet, God is not finished." Remember that on your journey, every misstep and every triumph plays a vital role, molding you into the person God created you to be. So rest in His love, align yourself with His purpose, and let the fear of failure dissipate in the face of His unbreakable promises.

Chapter 10
True Bravery:
Biblical Guidance to Overcome Your Fears

When you are in love with God, you are not afraid to yield your life to him. ~ Heidi Baker, Missionary to Africa

AS WE COME TO THE END of this book, although not the end of saying yes to Jesus, we must ask ourselves: what does true bravery look like for a follower of Christ? Whether we are in ministry, on the mission field, in the marketplace, or at home, we must know what living courageously looks like in our sphere of influence. True bravery is not the absence of fear, but rather the willingness to say yes to Jesus even when you are scared. It means taking risks and stepping out in faith, trusting that God is with you every step of the way.

Perhaps the most profound act of bravery we can demonstrate as Christians is to fully surrender our lives to Jesus Christ. This means acknowledging our own sinfulness and need for a savior, and trusting in His death and resurrection as the only means of salvation. It means allowing Him to transform us from the inside out, and being willing to follow Him wherever He leads, even if it means sacrificing our own desires or plans.

> In the end, true bravery is not about us at all—it is about Jesus.

In the end, true bravery is not about us at all—it is about Jesus. It is about trusting in His goodness, His faithfulness, and His love, and allowing Him to work through us for His purposes and His glory. May we all be inspired to live lives of true bravery, saying yes to Jesus even when we are scared, and trusting in

TRUE BRAVERY IS NOT THE ABSENCE OF FEAR, BUT RATHER THE WILLINGNESS TO SAY YES TO JESUS EVEN WHEN YOU ARE SCARED.

Him to guide us every step of the way.

Ultimately, authentic valor for a Christian means living a life that is fully surrendered to God, trusting in His goodness and sovereignty even in the midst of uncertainty or adversity. It indicates following Him wherever He leads and being willing to take risks and step out in faith, knowing that He will be with you, *"He will not leave you nor forsake you"* (Hebrews 13:5).

Throughout the Bible, there are numerous examples of individuals who demonstrated courage in the face of adversity, persecution, and even death. These examples can serve as a source of inspiration and encouragement for us as we seek to live lives of sincere boldness as followers of Jesus Christ.

One of the most well-known examples of bravery in the Bible is the story of David and Goliath. In 1 Samuel 17, we read about how the Philistines and the Israelites were preparing for battle, and how the Philistine giant, Goliath, taunted the Israelites and challenged them to send out a champion to fight him. David, a young shepherd boy, stepped forward to accept the challenge, despite being vastly outnumbered and outmatched. He faced Goliath with nothing but a slingshot and a stone, but he had faith in God and trusted in His strength and protection. In verse forty five, David declares to Goliath:

You come against me with sword and spear and javelin, but I come against you in the name of the Lord Almighty, the God of the armies of Israel, whom you have defied. (NIV)

...trust and dependence on God are what allows us as Christians to be valiant in the face of our challenges and difficulties.

David's bravery in this story was not rooted in his abilities or strength but rather in his trust in God. He knew that God was with him and would fight for him, even against an opponent as formidable as Goliath. This same trust and dependence on God are what allows

us as Christians to be valiant in the face of our challenges and difficulties.

Another example of true courage in the Bible is the story of
Shadrach, Meshach, and Abednego, who refused to bow down to
the golden image that King Nebuchadnezzar had set up. In Daniel
3, we read about how the three men were thrown into a fiery furnace as punishment for their disobedience. But even in the face of
death, they refused to compromise their faith and worship anything
or anyone other than God. In verse seventeen, they declare to the
king:

*If we are thrown into the blazing furnace, the God we serve is able
to deliver us from it, and He will deliver us from Your Majesty's hand.
(NIV)*

God indeed delivered Shadrach, Meshach, and Abednego from
the fiery furnace. Their bravery in the face of persecution and death
serves as a powerful example of what it means to stand firm in your
faith, even when it is difficult or unpopular.

In the New Testament, we see numerous examples of people
unleashing their bravery among the early Christians who faced persecution and opposition for their beliefs. In Acts 5, we read about
how the apostles were arrested and imprisoned for preaching the
gospel, but an angel of the Lord opened the prison doors and set
them free. When the high priest and the council questioned them
about their disobedience, Peter boldly declared in verse 29:

We must obey God rather than human beings! (NIV)

The apostles' courage in this story reminds us that our ultimate
allegiance is to God, even if it means facing persecution or opposition from those around us. We are called to be obedient to Him
above all else, and to trust in His protection and provision even in
the face of adversity.

Perhaps the ultimate example of valor in the Bible is Jesus Christ,
who willingly laid down His life for the sake of others. In John 15:13

NIV, Jesus declares, *"Greater love has no one than this: to lay down one's life for one's friends."* Jesus demonstrated true bravery in His willingness to go to the cross, knowing that it would mean bearing humanity's sins and enduring God's wrath. But His sacrifice ultimately brought salvation and redemption. Jesus' courage gave us the gift of eternal life.

> Perhaps the ultimate example of valor in the Bible is Jesus Christ, who willingly laid down His life for the sake of others.

What can your bravery bring to this world? What can my valor bring to this world? Because my faith building days are not over, I am sure there will be a lot more yesses along the way. I have learned so much about being brave with these two decades on the mission field. I am sure I will recount more of God's story of bravery as I continue

> Jesus' courage gave us the gift of eternal life.

to say yes to Him. I hope you will too.

I want to leave you with ten ways you can overcome fear and be brave as you say yes to Jesus.

1. Trust in God's promises: The Bible repeatedly tells us to trust God's promises, even when we are afraid. In Isaiah 41:10 NIV, God says, *"Do not fear, for I am with you; do not be dismayed, for I am your God. I will strengthen you and help you; I will uphold you with my righteous right hand."* When we trust in God's promises, we can find the courage to face our fears.

2. Seek God's guidance: Proverbs 16:9 NIV says, "In their hearts humans plan their course, but the LORD establishes their steps." And Psalms 32: 8 NIV says: "I will instruct you and teach you in the way you should go; I will counsel you with my loving eye on you." When you seek God's guidance and submit to His will, you can find clarity and direction in the face of fear and uncertainty.

3. Maintain an attitude of gratitude: Philippians 4:6-7 NIV tells us, "*Do not be anxious about anything, but in every situation, by prayer and petition, with thanksgiving, present your requests to God. And the peace of God, which transcends all understanding, will guard your hearts and your minds in Christ Jesus.*" When you pray and give thanks, God removes your fears, and places His peace in you. You can find peace and courage amid fear.

4. Remember God's faithfulness: When we face fear and uncertainty, it can be easy to forget God's past faithfulness. However, the Bible reminds us of God's faithfulness repeatedly. In Psalm 34:4 NIV, we are told, "*I sought the Lord, and he answered me; he delivered me from all my fears.*" When we remember God's faithfulness, we can find comfort and strength in knowing that He is with us, even when we are scared.

5. Focus on love, not fear: 1 John 4:18 NIV says, "*There is no fear in love. But perfect love drives out fear, because fear has to do with punishment. The one who fears is not made perfect in love.*" When we focus on God's love for us and our love for others, we can find the courage to overcome fear. Rather than focusing on your own fears and limitations, you can focus on how you can love and serve others despite your angst. By turning your attention outward and seeking to show God's love to others, you can find the strength to face your fears and live courageously.

6. Meditate on God's Word: Psalm 119:114 NIV says, "*You are my refuge and my shield; I have put my hope in your word.*" When we meditate on God's Word, we can find comfort, wisdom, and strength to face our fears. You can also find examples of how God has helped others overcome their fears throughout the Bible.

7. Surrender to God's will: Jesus himself teaches us to surrender to God's will in the face of fear. In Matthew 26:39 NIV, he says, "*My Father, if it is possible, may this cup be taken from me. Yet not as I will, but as you will.*" By surrendering to God's will, we can find the courage to face our fears, knowing that God's plan for our lives is greater than our own. This means, doing what God has called you to do, even if you are scared. Just do it afraid.

8. Build resilience through adversity: Romans 5:3-4 NIV says, *"Not only so, but we also glory in our sufferings, because we know that suffering produces perseverance; perseverance, character; and character, hope."* When we face adversity and overcome it with God's help, we can build resilience and grow in our faith. We can also look back on these experiences as evidence of God's faithfulness in helping us overcome our apprehensions.

9. Trust in God's power, not your own: In 2 Corinthians 12:9 NIV, Paul writes, "But *he said to me, 'My grace is sufficient for you, for my power is made perfect in weakness.' Therefore, I will boast all the more gladly about my weaknesses, so that Christ's power may rest on me."* Rather than relying on our own strength, we can trust in God's power to help us overcome our fears. By admitting our weaknesses and surrendering to God's power, we can find the courage and strength we need to face even our greatest fears.

10. Remember that God is with you: In Joshua 1:9 NIV, God tells Joshua, *"Have I not commanded you? Be strong and courageous. Do not be afraid; do not be discouraged, for the Lord your God will be with you wherever you go."* Just as God was with Joshua as he faced his challenges, so God is with us in our times of fear and uncertainty. By remembering that God is with us always, we can find the courage to face our fears and trust in His plan for our lives.

...living bravely is not living fearlessly. It is saying yes to Jesus even when we are scared and trusting in God's strength and guidance.

Friends, living bravely is not living fearlessly. It is saying *yes* to Jesus even when we are scared and trusting in God's strength and guidance. As we have seen, there are many people in the Bible who have overcome fear. There are many biblical references to help us. These include trusting in God's promises, seeking His guidance, praying for strength, remembering His faithfulness, focusing on love, meditating on His Word, surrendering to His will, building resilience through adversity, seeking the Holy Spirit's guidance, and trusting in God's strength when we are weak. By putting these principles into practice in our lives, we can unleash our bravery and become the courageous people God created us to be. He is always with us and we can do all things through Him

> There is no retiring from building His Kingdom.

who gives us strength (Philippians 4:13). May we all have the courage to say yes to Jesus, even when we are scared, and live boldly and bravely in the knowledge that we are loved and guided by the One who created us.

I wonder where my next yes will lead, because I know my faith building days are not over. I want to continue to go all-in with God's plans for my life and ministry for the rest of my days. There is no retiring from building His Kingdom. The future is unknown, and can be scary, but I can boldly pro-

> In Christ I am brave. In Christ I am courageous

claim: In Christ I am brave. In Christ I am courageous because I know the Lord my God will be with me, even when I tremble with fear. I pray that you, my brave friend, will have many more yesses in you for Jesus. It is time to unleash your bravery, wherever God may lead you.

ABOUT THE AUTHOR

Heidi Elizarraraz is renowned for her gift of inspiring and nurturing unwavering faith in others.

Heidi pursued higher education at the University of California, Santa Barbara, graduating with a double major in Spanish and Communications, complemented by a minor in Latin American Studies. Her thirst for language and culture led her to Granada, Spain, where she immersed herself in Spanish.

Little did she anticipate that her path would lead her to Mexico as a missionary. In 2003, during a transformative mission trip to the orphanage formerly known as Rancho De Sus Niños, Heidi experienced a profound encounter with God. His call into full-time ministry in Mexico marked the beginning of her extraordinary journey. What began as a commitment of one year has blossomed into two decades of dedicated service to Him.

It was at this orphanage that she crossed paths with Daniel, her future husband. In 2005, they were married, and just two days after their wedding, they embarked on a remarkable venture, founding Open Arms Childcare Ministries in the quaint pueblo of La Misión. Armed with only $1, abundant faith, and a plethora of fears, they embraced Jesus' call to keep families together through no-cost childcare centers in Baja California, Mexico.

Their dedication bore fruit with the opening of a second campus in Camalú in 2017, accompanied by the establishment of Open Arms Church, where they served as founding pastors. Heidi's pursuit of theological knowledge led her to return to school, traveling tirelessly to Tijuana once a month, culminating in her graduation as Summa Cum Laude.

Despite her initial trepidation, Heidi discovered profound

fulfillment in pastoral ministry, a testament to God's guiding hand. Together with Daniel, she oversees three childcare campuses, providing a refuge for vulnerable children, and has planted three churches in Mexico and Cuba.

An esteemed bilingual speaker on the international stage, Heidi empowers audiences to embrace courage and wholeheartedly say yes to Jesus even if they are afraid. In this, her first book, she recounts her remarkable odyssey and inspires readers to embark on their own transformative journey.

To learn more or to support our mission, please visit:
OpenArmsMexico.org

You can also connect with the author at:
UnleashYourBravery.com

STEP-BY-STEP GUIDE FOR SALVATION

Step 1: Acknowledge Your Need for Salvation

Recognize that everyone falls short of God's perfect standard (Romans 3:23). Acknowledge your own sinfulness and the separation it causes between you and God (Isaiah 59:2).

Step 2: Understand God's Love and Plan of Salvation

Understand that God loves you and desires a relationship with you. Recognize that God provided a solution for sin through Jesus Christ who came to save you (John 3:16, Romans 5:8).

Step 3: Repent and Turn to God

Repentance involves a genuine sorrow for sin and a willingness to turn away from it. Confess your sins to God, seeking His forgiveness (Acts 3:19, 1 John 1:9).

Step 4: Believe in the Lordship of Jesus Christ

Believe in Jesus as the Son of God and the Savior of the world. Acknowledge His death on the cross as payment for your sins and His resurrection as a demonstration of His power over sin and death (John 14:6, Romans 10:9).

Step 5: Invite Jesus into Your Life

Invite Jesus Christ to be the Lord and Savior of your life. Surrender control to Him, trusting in His grace for salvation (Revelation 3:20).

Step 6: Confess Jesus as Lord

Confess with your mouth that Jesus is Lord and believe in your heart that God raised Him from the dead. This public declaration is an expression of your faith (Romans 10:9-10).

Step 7: Receive the Gift of Salvation

Understand that salvation is a gift from God that cannot be earned through good deeds. Receive God's grace and the gift of eternal life through faith in Jesus Christ (Ephesians 2:8-9).

Step 8: Begin a Relationship with God

Develop a personal relationship with God through prayer, reading the Bible, and participating in a local Christian community. Allow the Holy Spirit to guide and transform your life (James 4:8, 2 Timothy 3:16-17).

Step 9: Continue in Faith

Christianity is a journey. Continue to grow in your faith, seeking to follow Jesus in every aspect of your life. Trust in God's promises and allow Him to lead you (Colossians 2:6-7).

Step 10: Share Your Faith

As you experience the transformative power of God's love, share your faith with others. Be a witness to the grace and salvation found in Jesus Christ (Matthew 28:19-20, Acts 1:8).

Remember that salvation is a personal and transformative experience. This guide serves as a general outline, and individual experiences may vary. If you have questions or concerns, consider seeking guidance from a trusted pastor, a Christian mentor, or a local church community.

STUDY GUIDE

Chapter 1
BE STRONG AND COURAGEOUS: Facing Your Fears

1. Reflect on Joshua 1:9 (NIV)
- What does being "strong and courageous" mean in your faith journey?
- How does this verse apply to facing fear and uncertainty?

2. Personal Reflection
- Share a moment when you felt a strong call to step out of your comfort zone.
- How did God speak to you, and how did you respond?

3. The Crossroads
- Explore the author's crossroads moment.
- Have you experienced a similar situation?
- How can you actively listen for God's guidance in life-altering decisions?

4. Dealing with Fear
- Discuss the author's description of fear as a "paralyzing sensation."
- Share a time when you overcame fear to say yes to God.

5. Defeating Border Bullies
- Explore the concept of "border bullies" as obstacles to God's plan.
- Have you encountered similar challenges?

- How can lessons from the Israelite spies' story apply to over-coming doubts and negativity?

6. Kicking Fear in the Face

- Reflect on the author's statement, "I've discovered that some-times I just have to do it scared."
- List practical steps to kick fear in the face and move forward in faith.

7. Closing Reflection

- Consider the author's journey. How does her story encourage you in your pursuit of God's calling?
- What steps can you take to unleash your bravery and say yes to Jesus, even in the midst of fear?

Chapter 2
ALL-IN: Fear of Inadequacy

1. Fear of Inadequacy

- Share a time when fear of inadequacy held you back from saying yes to God's call.
- What did you do, or what would you do differently?

2. The Temptation to Run

- Discuss the author's temptation to run back to comfort. In what areas of your life do you feel tempted to choose comfort over God's calling?
- How can you overcome the temptation to run when faced with unexpected and challenging circumstances?

3. Lessons from Psalm 56:3-4

- Explore how the author clung to Psalm 56:3-4 during times of fear. How can this scripture be applied in our lives when facing uncertainties?
- Share personal experiences where trusting God helped you overcome fear.

4. Lessons from the Refining Fire

- What is the "refining fire"?
- Have you experienced a refining fire in your life that strengthened your faith?

5. All-In Commitment

- Reflect on the call to go all-in for Jesus. How does this commitment transcend specific roles or occupations?
- Share examples of individuals you know or who are well-known, who embody an all-in commitment to following God's call on their lives.
- What fears or hesitations do you need to overcome to live an all-in life for Jesus?
- Are you ready to go all-in with God's plans and calling for your life?

6. Closing Reflection

- Summarize how this chapter encourages you to confront fears of inadequacy and embrace an all-in commitment to God.
- Share specific steps you can take to live an all-in kind of faith in your daily life.

Chapter 3
ARE YOU WILLING? The Power to Rise Above Fear

1. Reflecting on Personal Fear

- As the author faced fear in her own journey, she discovered the power to rise above it. Reflect on a moment in your life when fear loomed large, hindering your obedience to God's call.
- How did you navigate that fear, and what did you learn about the relationship between fear and faith?

2. Divine Purpose Amidst Uncertainty

- The story of Rebekah in Genesis 24 reveals the unfolding of God's divine purpose amidst uncertainty. Discuss a time in your life when you had to step into the unknown, trusting in God's purpose even when the outcome was unclear.
- How did God reveal His plan to you?

3. Freedom of Choice and Consequences

- The story of Rebekah emphasizes freedom of choice but also highlights the lack of freedom from consequences. Share a personal experience where you had to make a choice, understanding that there would be consequences.
- How did this choice impact your life, and what did you learn from it?

4. God's Will and Obedience

- Explore the concept of discerning God's will, as mentioned in John 6:40 and Mark 16:15. How do these verses speak to the responsibility of believers to align themselves with God's will and to participate in fulfilling His purposes on earth?
- How does obedience play a role in this?
- Are you willing to make Jesus' last command your first priority?

5. Saying *Yes* to God's Call

- The author shares her own experiences of saying yes to Jesus even in the face of fear. Reflect on a specific instance in your life where you had to say yes to God's call despite fear or uncertainty.
- Did fear win or did you unleash your bravery?

6. The Impact of Choices on God's Plan

- Consider the profound impact of Rebekah's choice on God's plan affecting the lineage of Jesus. Have you ever made a decision that you realized impacted your future generations?
- How do our individual choices contribute to or hinder God's plan in our lives and in the lives of others?

7. The Power of Prayer and Faith

- The chapter emphasizes the power of prayer and faith in the face of financial challenges. Share instances from your life where prayer and faith played a crucial role in overcoming obstacles.
- How can believers cultivate a deeper trust in God's provision, especially when faced with seemingly insurmountable circumstances?

8. Overcoming Fear and Doubt

- The narrative portrays a moment of fear and doubt when the author and her husband had only $1. Share a personal experience where fear and doubt threaten to derail your trust in God's plan.
- How did you overcome these challenges, and what role did faith play in navigating through uncertainties?

9. Impact of Willingness on God's Plan

- The chapter draws parallels between Rebekah's willingness to leave her family and homeland and the author's willingness to embrace God's call. Discuss the impact of human willingness on the fulfillment of God's plan.

- How does your own willingness to say yes to God contribute to His purposes in your life and the lives of others?
- Are you willing to unleash your bravery and say yes to Jesus, even if you are afraid?

Chapter 4
THE GOD OF THE 11TH HOUR:
Fear That God Is Insufficient

1. Trusting in God's Sufficiency
- Reflect on a time in your life when you faced a situation that seemed insurmountable. How did you navigate feelings of doubt and uncertainty?
- What role did your trust in God's sufficiency play in overcoming those challenges?

2. Redefining Orphan Care
- Consider your perspective on orphan care. How does the chapter challenge or reshape your understanding of this concept?
- What are some other ways in which individuals, churches, or communities can contribute to preventing child abandonment while promoting family preservation?
- Examine the statistics and studies presented regarding the consequences of institutionalizing children. How does this information impact your views on traditional orphan care methods?
- What specific steps can you take to contribute to the fight for families and prevent unnecessary separation of children from their parents?

3. Embracing Eleventh-Hour Miracles

- Share a personal experience where you felt God's intervention at the last moment, akin to an eleventh-hour miracle. How did this experience shape your faith and trust in God's timing?
- Discuss how embracing a perspective of trusting God's provision can impact your daily life.
- The chapter provides practical steps to experience eleventh-hour miracles, including rejoicing, continual prayer, gratitude, and reliance on the Holy Spirit. How can you incorporate these principles into your daily routine to strengthen your faith and reliance on God?

4. Challenging Fear and Doubt

- Fear and doubt often hinder our ability to trust in God's sufficiency. Reflect on a current fear or doubt you may be facing.
- How can the principles shared in the chapter, particularly the verses from Psalm 34:4-8, guide you in overcoming these fears and deepening your trust in God?

Chapter 5
FAITH MAKES MIRACLES POSSIBLE:
Fear of Leaving Your Comfort Zone

1. Defining Comfort Zone

- How would you define leaving one's comfort zone in the context of faith?
- Why is leaving your comfort zone crucial for witnessing miracles?

2. Personal Faith Activation

- Can you recall a personal experience where faith was activated in moments of fear?

- How did saying yes to God's call play a role in overcoming challenges?

3. Impact of Collective Faith
- Discuss the significance of collective faith, as seen in the children's contribution to Heidi Baker's ministry.
- Have you ever believed God for something with others? What was the outcome?

4. Facing Opposition
- Reflect on the author's journey to plant their second campus in Camalú despite warnings from another Christian not to go there. People may have good intentions, but God's plan will always prevail. What do you think you would have done after hearing that news?
- How does this resonate with biblical stories of resilience in the face of opposition?

5. Living a Life of Radical Love
- Reflect on the connection between 1 John 3:1 and the author's commitment to live a life marked by radical love.
- How does a deep love for Jesus correlate with trust in His plans, even when they seem overwhelming?

6. Prayer and Miraculous Provision
- Explore the significance of the author's prayer for reassurance and the specific request for a sign of God's provision. Has God ever been so clear to you, that you had to say *yes* to His plans, even if you were scared? Explain.
- How did obedience to God's prompting lead to a miraculous act of generosity?

7. Dependence on God Alone

- Reflect on the author's call to depend on God alone for everything. Can you identify instances in your life where dependence on worldly resources may have hindered you from seeing miracles?
- How can a shift in dependence impact your faith?

Chapter 6
NO! I CAN'T GO! Fear of Losing Control

1. Reflecting on Fear of Losing Control

- Have you ever experienced fear of losing control in your life?
- What situations triggered this fear, and how did it affect you emotionally and mentally?

2. Faith vs. Control

- The quote by Mark Batterson states, "You can have faith or you can have control, but you cannot have both." What does this mean to you personally?
- How do faith and control intersect or conflict in your life?

3. Biblical Reflection—Moses

- Explore the story of Moses and the Israelites in the desert (Numbers 11). How did Moses respond when faced with challenges beyond his control?
- What can we learn from his reliance on God in moments of overwhelming responsibility?

4. Personal Struggles with control

- The author talks about adopting the belief that control provides security. Can you relate to this in your life?
- How has the fear of losing control impacted your decisions and relationships?

- Can you identify with the internal struggle of letting go, especially when it involves something deeply personal or significant?

5. Dangers of Control—King David's Story
- Discuss King David's story with Bathsheba and Uriah, and how his desire for control led to significant mistakes.
- How did David's control issues impact his decisions, and what were the consequences?

6. Letting Go of Control
- The book suggests biblical steps for letting go of control. Which of these steps (acknowledging God's ultimate control, presenting fears to God, trusting in God's plan, seeking His will, releasing perfectionism) resonates with you the most?
- Reflect on a time when your need for control affected others negatively. How did this experience shape your understanding of control and its impact on relationships?

7. Personal Growth
- Share instances in your life where letting go of control led to personal growth or positive outcomes.
- How did surrendering control impact your relationship with God and others?

8. Embracing the Unknown
- The author speaks of embracing the unknown with courage. How do you approach uncertainties in life?
- What role does faith play in facing the unknown?
- Take time to reflect on one area in your life where you struggle to let go of control. How can you apply the biblical principles discussed in the chapter to surrender control in that area?

Chapter 7
MY GREATEST FEAR: Fear of Being Out of God's Will

1. Reflecting on Fear of Being Out of God's Will
- Share a personal experience when you resisted God's call or direction.
- How did fear play a role in your initial response?
- How can fear sometimes disguise itself as other emotions, such as anger or insecurity, impacting our decisions?

2. Exploring the Attitude of Gratitude
- Discuss the significance of adopting an attitude of gratitude, especially in times of fear and uncertainty.
- How has gratitude played a role in your life in fostering trust in God and overcoming challenges?

3. Seeking Confirmation
- Heidi sought a sign from God similar to Gideon. Share instances where you sought confirmation or guidance from God.
- How do you balance seeking signs with walking in faith?

4. Reflecting on Mary Magdalene's Boldness
- How can Mary Magdalene's boldness inspire us to step into our callings, even when societal norms may challenge our credibility?
- How does it make you feel that Jesus chose a woman to entrust with the gospel message?
- Are you willing to "Go and Tell" (Mathew 28:7)? Write down one person you will witness to this week and invite them to church.

5. Personal Application
- Confronting Fears: Identify and confront specific fears or

uncertainties hindering your journey. Write down some fears you are facing today.

- How might acknowledging these fears pave the way for embracing God's will?
- Embracing God's Call: Reflect on instances of resisting God's call. How can you align yourself more closely with God's will, even in the face of fear and uncertainty?

6. Action Steps

- Prayer and Petition: Bring fears and uncertainties before God in prayer, following the model of Philippians 4:6-7.
- Gratitude Challenge: Encourage the practice of gratitude daily for a week and share experiences at the next study.
- Courageous Steps: Identify one area in your life where you feel God calling you and take a courageous step, trusting in God's strength.
- Encouragement Cards: Write an encouragement card to someone facing a difficult decision or a fear. Share these cards with the group.

Chapter 8
TRAGEDY, LOSSES, AND HEARTACHE:
Fear of Not Being Enough

1. Courageous Love Beyond Outcomes

- In this chapter the author changes directions, and talks vulnerably about tragedy, loss, and heartache. The mission field, and your life are not always filled with Instagrammable moments. What have you learned about courageous love from these stories?
- It is easy to throw in the towel, when unexpected circumstances and outcomes arise. How can you continue to have faith, hope, and love despite trying times?

2. Dealing with Failure and Inadequacy

- The author expresses feelings of failure and inadequacy in certain situations. Share a personal experience where you faced failure or felt inadequate.
- How did you cope with these feelings?
- Consider the perspective that the true mark of courage is not in never falling down but in getting back up and trying again. How can this perspective shape your approach to challenges?

3. The Role of Comfort and Compassion

- Examine the role of comfort and compassion in the face of tragedy. Have you ever gone through a tragedy where someone offered compassion towards you? How did this make you feel?
- Share your thoughts on the significance of comforting those who mourn, as mentioned in Matthew 5:4, and how it aligns with the Christian understanding of community and shared burdens.

4. Finding Jesus in Pain and Loss

- The author acknowledges the difficulty of sharing stories of hardship and loss. Have you ever gone through hardships or loss, and found Jesus or even came to know Him more deeply?
- How do you reconcile the idea of God's goodness in the face of tragic circumstances?

5. Anchoring Hope in Jesus

- What does anchoring your hope in Jesus mean to you when the storms come blowing at you in life? See Hebrews 6:18-19
- What does it mean to "not grow weary of doing good" for you, and your yes to Jesus?
- How can you maintain hope when faced with the fear of inadequacy, failure, or the unknown?

Chapter 9
IF IT'S NOT GOOD, GOD'S NOT DONE: Fear of Failure

1. Divine Orchestration

- Proverbs 16:9 says, *"In their hearts humans plan their course, but the Lord establishes their steps."* How does this verse align with the events in Chapter 9, particularly regarding the convergence of paths and the encounter with the couple who lost their daughters in a house fire?
- Reflect on instances in your life where you've seen evidence of divine orchestration. How did those experiences impact your faith?

2. Trusting God's Timing

- Read Psalm 27:13-14. How does the author's experience resonate with the psalmist's call to "wait patiently for the Lord" and to "be brave and courageous"?
- Share personal experiences where waiting on the Lord led to a deeper understanding of His goodness.

3. The Fear of Failure

- Galatians 1:10 says, *"Obviously, I'm not trying to win the approval of people, but of God. If pleasing people were my goal, I would not be Christ's servant."* How does the fear of failure hinder our ability to serve God wholeheartedly, as mentioned in the chapter?
- Share your own struggles with the fear of failure and discuss how prioritizing God's approval over human approval can alleviate this fear.

4. Resurrection Power

- Read John 11:5-7, 17. How does the story of Lazarus parallel the challenges faced in the Los Pinos endeavor? In what ways did God manifest His glory through waiting?

- Discuss instances in your life where you've witnessed God's resurrection power in seemingly hopeless situations.

5. If It's Not Good Yet, God's Not Done

- Reflect on the overarching message of the chapter: "If it's not good yet, God's not done." How can this perspective influence your approach to challenges and waiting on God?
- Is there something in your life, right now, that is not yet good? With the new perspective that God isn't done yet in your life and in your circumstances, how can you be brave today and trust God that He is still working?

Chapter 10
TRUE BRAVERY:
Practical Guidance to Overcome Your Fears

1. Personal Experience

- Share a personal experience where you had to overcome fear or activate true bravery in your faith journey.
- Reflect on a moment in your faith journey when saying yes to Jesus required you to take risks and to step out in faith despite feeling scared. How did God's presence and guidance make a difference?

2. Definition of True bravery

- Define what true bravery means to you when you step out to follow Jesus.
- Explore the idea that authentic valor for a Christian is rooted in complete surrender to God, trusting in His goodness and sovereignty. How does this perspective transform the way we face uncertainty or adversity?

3. Ten Ways to Overcome Fear

- Select one of the ten ways mentioned in the chapter (e.g., trusting in God's promises, seeking God's guidance, etc.). How can you implement this principle in your life to overcome the fears you are facing?
- Share a personal testimony or example of how relying on one of these principles helped you overcome fear.

4. Unleashing your Bravery Today

- Identify a current situation where God is calling you to step out in faith. What specific steps can you take to unleash your bravery in response to His call?
- Consider a time when remembering God's faithfulness was crucial in facing fear. How does recalling God's past faithfulness contribute to trust and courage in the present?
- How can you practically live bravely in your current circumstances, whether in ministry, at work, or at home?
- Share examples of how true bravery might look in your sphere of influence.

It all comes down to this: How can you unleash your bravery as a follower of Christ, as you say yes to Jesus, even when you are afraid?

NOTES

Chapter 1: Be Strong and Courageous: Facing Your Fears

1. "Fear." The Oxford English Dictionary. Oxford University Press, 2023. https://oed.com/search/dictionary/ ?scope=Entries&q =Fear
2. Wilkinson, Bruce. *The Dream Giver: Following Your God Given Destiny.* Multnomah Books, 2003

Chapter 2: All-In: Fear of inadequacy

1. *Not his real name

Chapter 3: Are You Willing?: The Power to Rise Above Fear

1. Hanes, Jack. *His Last Command Our First Priority.* Megalife Ministries, 2004.
2. Williamson, J. & Greenberg, A. (2010). *Families, Not Orphanages.* Working Paper, September 2010 https:// bettercarenetwork.org/library/particular-threats-to-childrens-care-and-protection/effects-of-institutional-care/families-not-orphanages

Chapter 4: The God of the 11th Hour: Fear That God Is Insufficient

1. Luna, Matilde (2010) Children and adolescents without parental care in Latin America: Contexts, causes and consequences of being deprived of the right to family and community life. https://relaf.org/Documento_Relaf.pdf

2. Smith, Rebecca (2018). *Orphanages Are Not The Solution.* https://savethechildren.org.uk/blogs/2018/volunteering-in-orphanages-not-solution-save-the-children-uk-blogs

3. *Information About Orphanages: Facts About Orphans & Statistics* (2018) https://rethinkorphanages.org/school-university-groups/information-about-orphanages-facts-about-orphans-statistics#:~:text=Globally%2C%20over%2080%25%20of%20children,to%20be%20living%20in%20orphanages.

4. Batha, Emma (2018). *Most Children in Orphanages Are Not Orphans.* https://reliefweb.int/report/world/most-children-orphanages-are-not-orphans

5. *Children in Latin America and the Carribean Overview 2020* https://unicef.org/lac/media/21911/file/NNAinLAC2020-one-page.pdf

6. *Why It Matters, Why Orphanages Harm Children* (2024) https://hopeandhomes.org/why-it-matters/how-orphanages-harm-children/

Chapter 5: Faith Makes Miracles Possible: Fear of Leaving Your Comfort Zone

1. Batterson, Mark. *Chase The Lion: If Your Dream Doesn't Scare You It's Too Small.* Multanmaoh, 2016.

2. "Encourage." Merriam-Webster Dictionary. 2024 https://merriam-webster.com/dictionary/encourage

Chapter 7: My Greatest Fear: Fear of Being Out God's Will

1. James D. G. Dunn, *Jesus Remembered* (Grand Rapids: Eerdmans, 2003), 832-33.

2. Leach, Tara Beth, *Emboldened: A Vision for Empowering Women in Ministry,* Intervarsity Press, pg. 17.

3. Bucher, Meg.(2022) *How Can Christians Be Strong and Courageous Like Deuteronomy 31 Says.* https://crosswalk.com/faith/bible-study/how-can-christians-be-strong-and-courageous-like-deuteronomy-31-says.html

4. Bloom, Jon (2016). *God Does Not Need You To Be Strong.* https://desiringgod.org/articles/god-does-not-need-you-to-be-strong

5. Bucher, Meg.(2022) *How Can Christians Be Strong and Courageous Like Deuteronomy 31 Says.* https://crosswalk.com/faith/bible-study/how-can-christians-be-strong-and-courageous-like-deuteronomy-31-says.html

Chapter 8: Tragedy, Loss, and Heart-Ache:Fear of Not Being Enough

1. *Not her real name
2. *Not his real name
3. *Not her real name

Chapter 9: If It's Not Good, God's Not Done:Fear of Failure

1. Winters, Lynn. Sermon preached at Iglesia Open Arms, Camalu. (2023)

To learn more or to support our mission, please visit:
OpenArmsMexico.org

You can also connect with the author at:
UnleashYourBravery.com

ABOOKS

ALIVE Book Publishing and ALIVE Publishing Group
are imprints of Advanced Publishing LLC,
3200 A Danville Blvd., Suite 204, Alamo, California 94507

Telephone: 925.837.7303
alivebookpublishing.com

Printed in the USA
CPSIA information can be obtained
at www.ICGtesting.com
LVHW020514120824
787858LV00005B/10

9 781631 322341